Counting IT ALL Joy

CHOOSING JOY OVER
PAINFUL CIRCUMSTANCES
WITH GOD'S HELP

LAURIE CLINE

Copyright © 2021 by **Laurie Cline**

Counting It All Joy

All rights reserved. No part of this publication may be reproduced, distributed, or transmitted in any form or by any means, including photocopying, recording, or other electronic or mechanical methods, without the prior written permission of the publisher, except in the case of brief quotations embodied in critical reviews and certain other noncommercial uses permitted by copyright law.

Although the author and publisher have made every effort to ensure that the information in this book was correct at press time, the author and publisher do not assume and hereby disclaim any liability to any party for any loss, damage, or disruption caused by errors or omissions, whether such errors or omissions result from negligence, accident, or any other cause.

Adherence to all applicable laws and regulations, including international, federal, state, and local governing professional licensing, business practices, advertising, and all other aspects of doing business in the US, Canada, or any other jurisdiction is the sole responsibility of the reader and consumer.

Neither the author nor the publisher assumes any responsibility or liability whatsoever on behalf of the consumer or reader of this material. Any perceived slight of any individual or organization is purely unintentional.

The resources in this book are provided for informational purposes only and should not be used to replace the specialized training and professional judgment of a health care or mental health care professional.

Neither the author nor the publisher can be held responsible for the use of the information provided within this book. Please always consult a trained professional before making any decision regarding treatment of yourself or others.

Cover Design: Britney Thompson, www.brenaedesignco.com
Interior Layout: Britney Thompson
Cover Photo: Pajor Pawel

ISBN: 978-0-578-83164-0

This book is dedicated to my husband Chris; I love you with all my heart and you are my hero. I also dedicate this book to my brother Jeff in heaven; you inspire me every day to follow my dreams.

"My brethren, count it all joy when ye fall into divers temptations; Knowing this, that the trying of your faith worketh patience."

— James 1:2–3 KJV

Table of Contents

INTRODUCTION

CHAPTER 1   Down in the Valley
CHAPTER 2   When It Rains, It Pours
CHAPTER 3   You Can't Make This Stuff Up
CHAPTER 4   A Slice of Humble Pie
CHAPTER 5   Prayer Quilt
CHAPTER 6   Mailbox Money
CHAPTER 7   A Blessing in the Storm
CHAPTER 8   A Hard Goodbye
CHAPTER 9   You Can't Pour From an Empty Cup
CHAPTER 10   Find Your Joy
CHAPTER 11   Gratitude Changes the Attitude
CHAPTER 12   Amazing Grace

ACKNOWLEDGMENTS

ABOUT THE AUTHOR

Introduction

I am so thankful for God's mercy and grace. I have spent some wonderful times in my life on the mountaintop with God, and I savor those beautiful memories. The mountaintop is a grand view of life where things seem almost perfect. But everything that goes up must come down. Our family was suddenly knocked off that beautiful mountaintop and plunged deep into the valley like an airplane falling out of the sky. When we looked around to survey the damage from our fall, we were as low as you can go in the pit of despair. Nothing resembled our old life.

I struggled for years with the pain and scars of watching my once healthy husband become completely disabled. It consumed me to the point that my once seemingly rock-solid, unshakeable faith was, well… shaken. My heart knew that God was good and that my circumstances didn't dictate His goodness, yet our crash landing from the mountaintop to the slimy pit of despair was devastating.

That was eight years ago, and I am not even the same person today. Watching people you love suffer changes you. I grappled with it for a long time. Life seemed so unfair, and at times I questioned God on how good could come from our tragic circumstances. The devil went hard after my family, and you know that to be true when people around you start comparing your life to the book of Job.

I struggled with what to do with all of the pain and sorrow as the chapters of this book scrolled through my head night after night. I questioned God on many occasions and even said out loud, "God, I am nobody, why would someone want to read my story?"

The Lord gave me such a strong impression that He would use my pain to help others if I would be willing to take a leap of faith to tell our story. There are many parts of our journey that are hard to retell. My goal in writing this book is to share our family's struggles through many hard trials to show you how we overcame them by making a conscious decision each day, even on the bad days, to choose joy over our hard circumstances.

My expectation is that you will find hope and encouragement from this book. Our stories are different, yet we have all had times in our lives when our faith has been tested beyond what we thought we could stand. We have all heard it said that God will not give you more than you can handle. I disagree. My hard season taught me that God will give more than you can handle so that you will turn to Him to find your strength. Nothing is too hard for God.

I am so thankful that you are here. Whether you are a person of strong faith, someone whose faith is being tested, or even someone questioning their faith or who doesn't believe, I hope that my story helps you consider God and His goodness. If you are tired and weary from the battle, I pray you find the strength to keep going. Life is hard and God is good, even when our circumstances seem like they will never get better. We can trust that God will see us through.

Counting it All Joy

Chapter 1

DOWN IN THE VALLEY

Eight years ago, my faith felt pretty solid. My life was far from perfect or problem free, but the good times definitely outweighed the bad. Our family had seen its fair share of heartbreak over the years, but you might say we were in the calm before the storm. Life was good.

Our walk through the valley began at the end of 2013. My husband and I had been married for almost twenty years, and our two boys were sixteen and twelve at the time. We were coming off of a very busy but content season in life.

My husband worked in law enforcement and started his career right out of college. It was a tough job, and it definitely took its toll on his body. Over the years, he had accumulated a long list of on-the-job injuries, though he always seemed to bounce back. My husband loved his job and felt like he was making a difference.

Though the hours could be a little crazy, I was super supportive of my husband's career. His retirement was on the horizon, and I knew that our lives would settle down eventually. My job and our two boys kept me "in demand" on the home front. I have a very fulfilling career as well, though being a mom is my favorite job title.

Besides working in law enforcement, my husband is also a preacher. During the summer of that year, our family had spent a wonderful week alongside my husband as he helped preach in a revival. We spent our days and nights in spirit-filled church services getting our souls fed. The week had brought us all closer to God and reminded us of what was important.

At the beginning of that same year, my husband injured himself at work. He ended up needing surgery to repair two ruptured discs in his neck. This was his second cervical spine surgery; his first was back in 2006. This surgery went well; he healed up quickly and was soon back to work doing what he loved.

A few months later, while helping a victim at the scene of an accident, he reinjured his neck. My husband realized something was wrong as he began having strange symptoms but kept them to himself for several months. We had no idea how life-changing this last injury would be to all of our lives.

Within a short amount of time, the pain began to worsen, and my husband was struggling to keep his normal pace. After a trip to the ER, an MRI revealed more ruptured discs in his neck. Surgery was quickly scheduled for right after the New Year.

We arrived at the spine hospital early on January 8, 2014, for what we thought would be a routine surgery. My husband had been through this type of procedure twice before, and we knew the drill. After surgery, the nurses rolled him back into his room, and the doctor came in to give a report. He thought the surgery went well, though he admitted the damage was much more extensive than what he was expecting.

My husband had not only ruptured several discs in his neck, but he had also stripped screws that held the metal plates in place put in during his previous surgeries. This had caused vertebrae to splinter, and a small bone fragment was lodged in his spinal cord. The doctor told us he removed the piece of bone and had attempted to repair the damage.

Although the news was not what I expected to hear, I still had faith that my husband would be okay. He always seemed to push through in the past even though this injury was much more serious than his previous injuries. It had not registered in my mind yet that we were dealing with a spinal cord injury.

My husband has had a long list of surgeries over his lifetime. He was diagnosed with papilloma of the larynx when he was two years old and endured over forty vocal cord operations by the time he was in his early thirties. Over the years, he also had surgeries on his shoulder, knee, and both hands, plus a few other miscellaneous surgeries. The man has been in and out of hospitals his entire life, and I was clinging to the fact that he had always bounced back in the past. I was hoping this surgery would be no different.

After my husband began to wake up from the surgery, I noticed he was whispering instead of speaking in a normal voice. Honestly, I didn't think too much of it at first. It was not uncommon for him to be hoarse after surgery from being put to sleep. The alarm was not going off yet that there was a problem.

Thank goodness the doctor decided to keep him overnight for pain control. His first night was rough. The nurses had a difficult time getting him comfortable, and he suffered most of the night. His voice was still a faint whisper the next morning, so I asked him why he was still whispering. He said, "I can't talk." I responded with, "What do you mean you can't talk?" Worry was settling in my mind.

This was supposed to have been an outpatient surgery, but the next day my husband was still not showing signs of improvement and was actually worse. We ended up staying for two more days in the hospital. My husband was showing signs of severe neurological complications; this definitely wasn't turning out like we had expected.

After being home from the hospital a few days, we both started to realize that there were serious issues going on. He appeared to have suffered nerve damage from the spinal cord injury, and on top of that, his voice was not improving. His balance was completely off, and he was having trouble walking. He began using a walker to get around the house, thinking it would be temporary until his neck healed up.

On top of everything else, my husband had developed a tremor in his right hand and left foot. The toes on his left foot would flutter like a butterfly. This was not normal! I quickly made an appointment with the surgeon to find out what the heck was going on. The panic button was now pushed.

At our follow-up appointment, the doctor was perplexed as to why my husband was getting worse instead of better. The nerve damage was severe and obvious. My husband could not even hold a pen to sign his name; his right hand shook uncontrollably, like someone with Parkinson's.

The doctor seemed to completely ignore the fact that my husband's voice was still only a whisper. When I reminded the doctor of this, he quickly told us that it was a risk of this kind of surgery. Seriously? Maybe I was feeling a bit emotional, but I expected a little bit of sympathy. My husband and I were both frustrated that we were getting no answers.

We went to see my husband's ENT soon after, and he confirmed our worst fear. My husband's right vocal cord had been paralyzed during surgery. The doctor told my husband we needed to give it a good six months before we would know if the paralysis was permanent. Wait, did he just say permanent? As in, forever?

The ENT mentioned a procedure that could help with my husband's voice, but it was a temporary fix with no guarantees. Ugh, this was going from bad to worse. The last thing we wanted to hear was that he needed another surgery.

I became my husband's caretaker overnight along with keeping up with my existing responsibilities. I was trying to manage two kids, laundry, chores, doctors' appointments, and paying bills all while staying on top of my full time job. I honestly didn't know which way was up.

I had an area on the floor next to the side of my bed that became my altar. After my husband would fall asleep at night, I would slide out of bed and get on my knees in that spot and cry and beg God for help. Whose life was this anyway? I felt like I was living a nightmare I couldn't wake up from.

My husband needed assistance doing everything, and my sleep was constantly interrupted helping him through the night. It was a very scary and exhausting time, but I didn't feel justified to complain out loud. I was able to speak and walk, how could I dare complain that I was tired and overwhelmed?

I cried out to God so many days and nights during that first year for peace, for help, and for strength. I didn't want my family to see me upset, so I would cry in the shower, in my car, or after everyone else was asleep. I cried while folding laundry, feeding the dog, and walking to the mailbox. I felt so deep in the valley, and Jesus became so real to me.

It didn't matter what time it was, day or night, I knew that I could always pray and pour out my heart and soul. Sometimes it wasn't even an audible prayer. Unloading all my burdens on God became a part of my daily routine.

We were eventually referred to another neurosurgeon that took "worst case scenario" spine cases. After looking at my husband's MRI, the new doctor immediately scheduled another surgery to stabilize my husband's neck. Just five months from the surgery-gone-wrong, my husband was going into surgery number four on his neck.

I suppose in my mind, I still thought this new surgery would fix the problem. In reality, the new doctor was merely cleaning up the mess and trying to add stability. The damage to my husband's neck was irreversible, and his pain was horrific. After surgery, we spent three days in ICU and eleven more days in the hospital until he was stable enough to come home.

Chapter 1: Down in the Valley

Almost a year after my husband's first surgery, his application for disability was finally approved. Let me throw in a huge thank you Jesus! While it was heartbreaking to be forty-five years old and on full disability, it was a blessing and an answered prayer to finally have some money coming in. My husband had been out of work for almost a year, and the medical bills were staggering. I felt like I was drowning and dreaded the daily trip to the mailbox to see what new medical bill had arrived.

Each day became a challenge to survive. I can't even imagine all the thoughts that were running through my husband's mind. I was trying to appear strong for my family and stay positive. I wanted my kids to have some sort of normalcy and to feel like it was going to be okay. You have heard the old saying, "If mama ain't happy, then nobody is happy." That sort of applied here though it wasn't about happiness. I wanted to appear calm so that our kids would have reassurance that we were going to be okay.

Through all the hard moments, sleepless nights, worries, and fears, I learned how faithful God really is. No matter that I was a wreck; He never failed to show up when I needed Him the most. I knew God before this fiery trial, but after our lives fell apart, I felt like I got to know Him on a whole new level. Though my faith was being tested, I saw a different side of God that I had never experienced before. This was the beginning of my understanding God's true nature and His love for His children. "Letting go and letting God" was becoming my mantra.

2 Corinthians 4:8–9

"We are troubled on every side, yet not distressed; we are perplexed, but not in despair; Persecuted, but not forsaken; cast down, but not destroyed."

Chapter 2

WHEN IT RAINS IT POURS

By the end of 2014, we happily said good riddance to the worst year of our lives. We all had hopes for a better year. It had to get better, *right*? On top of my husband's surgeries, our oldest son had also seriously injured his knee a few months prior and had knee reconstruction surgery. He was recovering alongside his dad, so I had two patients to look after. We keep the hospitals in business, and I am only half kidding.

My husband's next surgery was already scheduled for January 23, 2015. His spine was a mess, and his lower back needed to be repaired. His neck was as good as it was going to get. Our thinking was that the lower back surgery would give him some much needed pain relief and stability.

Once again, we went into the surgery hopeful. After the surgery, we were back in the ICU for several days and then in the hospital for another week. Praise the good Lord for our extended family that stepped in and took care of our boys while I cared for my husband. I am also beyond grateful for the company I work for and my awesome boss. My company allowed me to put my family first; I was able to work remotely from the hospital or home—a true blessing!

Going to work became an escape for me. I was able to focus on things besides all of the sickness at home. I looked forward to my days in the office where I got to be a normal employee doing her job. It also allowed me to take a break from my caretaker role. As bad as that may sound, I needed to feel "normal" again.

Unfortunately, my husband's back surgery didn't end as expected. During the surgery or while in the hospital, my husband contracted a serious infection. He also came out of the surgery with paralysis in his left leg.

During this hospital stay, we also discovered my husband's throat problems went beyond not being able to speak. The paralyzed vocal cord was causing him to aspirate in his sleep. One night while lying on my cot in the hospital room, I woke up to horrible gurgling noises. I realized that my husband was choking in his sleep. I jumped up to hit the call button for the nurse and tried to wake him up.

The doctors decided to put him through swallow tests and feeding therapy while he was in the hospital. They figured out that thin liquids caused him to choke. We were introduced to "thickener" that had to go in all his liquids so he could swallow without choking. Yuck! We were told to keep a carbonated beverage on hand in case he choked on food.

We left the hospital with more disabilities than we came in with and went home exhausted and defeated. After about a week of being home, my husband started spiking fevers and having teeth chattering chills. Over the next few months, we went back to the surgeon and our family doctor multiple times. He was given antibiotics and told to come back if he didn't get better. This went on till the end of March. By this time, my husband had lost a noticeable amount of weight, ran a constant fever, slept most of the day, and was very weak and lethargic.

I didn't know what else to do. The doctors were not finding the root cause of his symptoms. Each day he would get a little worse. His surgeon finally ordered a scan of his back, and a pocket of fluid was found on the imaging at his incision site. My husband had an outpatient surgery soon after to remove the fluid, and once again we were told that everything looked fine.

I knew he was not okay; he was still running a constant fever and was going downhill fast. One day I was helping him get in the shower and it hit me like a ton of bricks how sick he really was. He looked like a concentration camp victim. He was literally skin and bones. The teeth chattering chills he had daily were so intense I was afraid he might break a tooth. He was *not* okay!

One Sunday afternoon, my mom came over to bring us lunch. She spent some time with my husband listening to him describe his symptoms. His appearance was shocking to others that did not see him every day. After she finished her visit with him, she took me in the other room and dropped the bomb. She told me she was afraid he was dying. Her words hung in the air like fog and felt like someone poured a bucket of cold water over my head.

My husband had shared with me a few nights before that he felt life leaving his body. Our youngest son also came to me in private and told me to please do something to help his Dad! It was a wake-up call, and I knew I had to get someone to listen. That night I prayed *hard* for God to get us to a doctor that would figure out what was going on before it was too late.

God answered. We went back to the neurosurgeon out of desperation, and he told us he had done all he knew to do. He decided to send my husband to an infectious disease doctor. Thankfully, we were able to get in quickly to see the new doctor. He would be the answer to our prayers. He listened attentively as we described all of my husband's symptoms and took swabs from my husband's incision that day to send off to the lab. Thank goodness my family pushed me to keep searching for answers.

My cell phone rang a few days later, and it was the infectious disease doctor calling me himself to give me the diagnosis. He told me to pack a bag and get my husband to the hospital ER to be admitted for surgery. My husband had not one but *two* strains of MRSA in his spine. For anyone that doesn't know, MRSA is a very resistant bacterial infection that can be hard to get rid of and can be very dangerous. My husband was on the verge of sepsis, and we had to move fast.

I hung up the phone and sat down for a quick, cleansing cry. I had known in my heart that there was something terribly wrong. As worried as I was about another surgery, I was thankful to finally have an answer. This new doctor would quickly become our hero and no doubt was a huge part of saving my husband's life.

I packed our bags, made arrangements for our kids, and drove us to the hospital an hour away from home. My husband was so sick and dehydrated; the nurses could not get an IV started. After two hours and thirteen sticks later, they finally gave up and decided to put in a central line during surgery. It was about 3:00 a.m. by this point, and we were both completely worn out.

My husband's regular surgeon was out on sabbatical that month, so a new surgeon was going to do the procedure. The plan was to reopen his back incision and clean out all the infection around his spine. He would also have a PIC line inserted in his arm, and we would administer IV antibiotics at home for six weeks.

The nurses weighed him prior to surgery; he was down sixty pounds from his normal weight. He was completely malnourished and at death's door, but praise the good Lord, he came through the surgery okay! We spent another week in the hospital, and then we were back at home where I had to learn how to take care of a PIC line.

My husband's medicine would arrive on our doorstep in a cooler. His medicine had to be refrigerated, but an hour before I put it in his PIC line, I had to let it warm up for thirty minutes, and each dose had to be exactly twelve hours apart. Home health came a few times a week to draw blood and send it off to a lab to check his levels. I messed up his doses a time or two and got his levels out of whack. This turned the six weeks into eight weeks. Did I mention that nursing is definitely not my calling?

The company I work for graciously allowed me to work at home again during this time. I am not sure that I would have been able to manage taking care of my husband and trying to make the long drive to my office. My boss told me to take care of my family first; he knew that I would get my work done.

I don't know if I can truly express my gratitude to my boss for letting me be at home. I was setting alarms all hours of the day for medicine and IVs; I had charts to track multiple medications and dosages. I also had to keep his wounds clean and bandages changed. Because of the MRSA, I had to be extra cautious. Being able to work from home eased the burden.

I learned that God is in the big things and the little things too. I kept a conversation with God going 24/7. I went to bed talking to God and woke up talking to God. He was my lifeline, and my sanity relied on the open communication line.

Everyone in my family pitched in. I think my parents were worried that I was carrying too heavy of a load trying to do it all. The last two years had been crazy. People were amazed that I stayed sane. I can tell you with zero hesitation, it wasn't me; it was *all* Jesus. I give Him all the credit and honor and glory. Everything around me was crumbling, but God had put peace in my heart and mind at that time that I can't even explain. I should have been a walking zombie, but instead I was steady and calm. It really makes no sense, but that is the power of prayer and our amazing God.

It was a very long year. Our oldest son graduated high school a month after my husband's surgery to clean out the infection in his back. My husband was still extremely sick, but he knew that it would break our son's heart if he missed graduation. The day before graduation, my husband told me he couldn't miss the ceremony; we needed to figure out a way to get him there.

We loaded my husband in a wheelchair and rolled him into the graduation. He was only able to stay long enough to see our son walk across the stage and receive his diploma before he left early to go back home to bed. Thankfully our last name is at the beginning of the alphabet, so our son was one of the first to walk the line.

During the ceremony, the speaker asked for all the parents to stand up for a round of applause for getting to this milestone. I stood up and held my husband's hand as he sat in his wheelchair and the tears began to fall. It was only because of God's mercy and grace that we were able to make it that day.

We could see our son's face from where we sat, and his smile said it all. Watching him look up in the stands beaming with pride was everything. I knew that even though he had not made a big fuss about his dad being there, it meant the world to see all of his family in the stands cheering him on.

The rest of that year was spent healing. My husband's disabilities had grown, and he required around-the-clock care. My in-laws and my husband's sister live just a few minutes away, and they would take turns staying with him while I worked. My mom was constantly coming by with groceries and food, and my dad and stepmom would pop in to check on us and break up the monotony of my husband being stuck in bed. Our boys always pitched in as well.

I could *not* have done it without the help of our friends and family. Our church family lifted us in prayer as well as other churches that my husband had preached at. We learned that local churches all around town had my husband on their prayer lists. We felt so grateful for those prayers, for the many cards and well wishes that were sent during that very uncertain time.

Sadly, many of my husband's friends, with the exception of a few, had all but disappeared. My heart hurt for him, but the good Lord sent a new "tribe" of friends that embraced him and carried us through a very tough time. If any of our "tribe" is reading this, I want to thank you from the bottom of my heart for taking the time to come to our house and helping us feel loved. Brother Leslie, thank you for your many visits and the strawberry milkshakes, they meant the world.

Life continued to humble us. Once again, at the end of 2015, we closed out the year hoping that 2016 would be better. It would definitely get more interesting. My husband was still healing but was officially over the MRSA infection. Bless this man's heart, he never complained. I am not sure I would have been as graceful if I had lived through all that the last two years had thrown at him.

My husband was basically bedridden and lived a pretty quiet existence from our bedroom. He still required round-the-clock care; he couldn't walk without assistance, and his voice was still a whisper. Talking on the phone was not an option because the person on the other end could not hear him. The disabilities took so much away from this once strong and vibrant man.

My husband couldn't even get dressed without help, talk about humbling. Our relationship grew stronger though even under the immense pressure. The Lord had faithfully carried us both in the storm. I wish I could say that it all ended there and everything went back to normal, but it didn't. We learned to accept our new reality with gratitude knowing that it could always be worse.

God showed up big for our family when we were at our very lowest. Our friends and family and even some strangers became the hands and feet of Jesus. The waves were crashing over our head day after day. Though God didn't stop the storm, He provided peace in the storm. It was a time in our life where we knew we should be down in the fetal position. Being in the valley with God grew our faith exponentially.

Psalm 126:5

"They that sow in tears shall reap in joy."

Counting it All Joy

Chapter 3

YOU CAN'T MAKE THIS STUFF UP

By 2016, we were pretty much living day-to-day. I didn't have time to look up from my hectic life. People would make comments to us that they thought our hard times would surely come to an end soon. Folks would say things like, "You guys have gone through so much, I know this next year will be better." I felt like the universe laughed out loud and said, "Hold my sweet tea honey, you ain't seen nothing yet!"

Our youngest son, who was now 14, had gone out to feed the dog one evening. As he was walking back to the house, he tripped and fell, landing on his shoulder. I heard the loud crash from in the house and came running to see what had just happened. I helped him in the house, and it was very obvious that he had hurt himself. His shoulder immediately started to swell up and was sticking up like a chicken wing.

Thankfully the next day we already had an appointment with my older son's orthopedic doctor, who specialized in knees and shoulders. The doctor's office agreed to see our youngest too. At the appointment, when the doctor came in and took one look at my son's shoulder, he sent him immediately for x-rays. The doctor's face told me all I needed to know—it was bad. If you can't see by now, our family doesn't do *anything* normal or easy.

The scariest part of my son's injury was the loss of feeling in his hand. He looked like he had a pillow stuffed under his shirt; his shoulder was swollen twice the size of his other one. His pain was intense and watching him suffer broke my heart.

My husband was still bedridden, so I was flying solo getting our son to appointments, though my husband was much better equipped to sympathize with our son with the pain and disruption of his life. My husband was well acquainted with pain and sorrow, and it seemed that God allowed him to comfort our son in ways that I couldn't.

A month later, our youngest became extremely ill one night. We thought it was a reaction from his shoulder pain or maybe even just a stomach bug. I gave him medicine for nausea and thought that "this too shall pass." A short time later, our son came to our bedroom doubled over with abdominal pain. I decided to google his symptoms and quickly realized that this might be an appendicitis attack. Oops!

I packed a quick bag and my son and I headed down to the children's hospital. He hung his head out of the passenger side window and threw up for most of the car ride to the hospital. It was insane! I put my flashers on and drove as fast as I could without going to jail.

The nurse got him back in triage as soon as we walked in the ER because he was *still* throwing up. I was beating myself up a little for missing the signs and symptoms initially. He was one sick puppy, and I just knew he had a ruptured appendix.

The nurses got his IV going with fluids and medicine to slow down the vomiting so they could take him for a CT scan. Surprisingly, the CT came back negative for appendicitis. I was relieved yet scratching my head wondering what in the world could make a human puke *that* many times. He ended up being admitted to the hospital for observation and stayed three days while doctor's poked and prodded trying to figure out why his stomach hurt so badly. In the end, they chalked it up to an infection and sent us home.

Less than twenty-four hours later, the puke-fest started up *again*! We tried all the home remedies but nothing worked. I hadn't even unpacked my bag from the first trip, so we grabbed bags, jumped in the car, and headed back to the hospital. This time it was more urgent. His abdominal pain was very intense and he was very weak. We walked into the ER, and they took him back immediately and started IV fluids. I was *convinced* it *had* to be appendicitis this time.

It got very busy in my son's ER room. He was severely dehydrated, so they were pumping fluids in him by manually squeezing the IV bag. They had given him medicine for pain, which was making his heart rate and oxygen levels drop. When they brought him back from the CT scan, I spent the next several hours sitting next to his bed watching his heart rate and oxygen like a hawk.

Every time my son's heart rate dropped too low, the alarms would go off and the nurse would come in the room and tell him to take deep breaths. I decided to help her out. It was the middle of the night and mama was tired. I leaned my chair back against the wall and put my feet on the side of the bed. When the alarms would sound, I would gently kick the bed and say loudly, "Breathe!" My son would take a deep breath, and the alarms would stop. This went on for hours.

Once again, the appendicitis test came back negative, but my son was too sick to send home. They admitted him to the hospital again for nausea and pain control, and they kept him four more days. We never got a good diagnosis, still chalking it up to an infection, but he was one sick kid and definitely needed medical attention.

During my son's hospital stay, his shoulder injury was still giving him grief. We mentioned his shoulder injury to the nurses, and they had a neurologist come examine him while we were there. The neurologist referred him to a neurosurgeon that specialized in this type of shoulder injury. I look back on this crazy week, and I can see that God was at work getting us where we needed to be. Maybe it was the long way around, but nonetheless, we were at least getting to the right place for his shoulder injury.

After four days, my son was released to go home and recover. He was given orders to eat a bland diet and take medicine to help with the nausea and stomach pain. Sometimes I wonder if this stomach adventure was God's way of getting *my* attention.

A few weeks later, I took him to his neurosurgeon appointment. His stomach was better, but his shoulder was still very swollen, and he had not regained full use of his hand. I was one worried mama. And did I mention that I was running on empty by this point?

The doctor came in the room and introduced himself. He examined my son's shoulder and setup physical therapy appointments with a hand therapist. Then I got

Chapter 3: You Can't Make this Stuff Up

the wind knocked out of me. The doctor asked me if anyone from the ER had gone over my son's CT scan on his abdomen and talked to me about the tumor on his lumbar spine. Wait, *what*?! Did he just say *tumor*? I barely caught the rest of what the doctor said and had to ask him to repeat our whole conversation. The doctor told us he hoped that it was benign and wanted to watch it for a few months and discuss at our next appointment. I felt like the world had stopped turning. He lost me at "tumor."

We left the appointment and went straight home. After my son had gone to his room, I went to our bedroom to tell my husband what had happened. Like me, he was also very worried. I needed to be alone, so I walked back to our spare bedroom to pray. Laying face down on the floor, I begged God for my son's life. I laid there for quite a while with terrible thoughts running through my mind. We had already been through so much with my husband's surgeries and health, please Lord, not our son! It seemed like someone had turned on the faucet and it would not turn off.

I shared the news with close family and asked for prayer for my son at church, but it was too hard for me to talk about. As difficult as it had been to watch my husband go through the tough things he had gone through, when it's your child, there is no comparison. Your kids are your heart, and when they hurt, you hurt.

I cried out to the Lord so many nights while we waited, quietly soaking my pillow with tears. I wanted to be strong for our son; I didn't want him to see the worry in my eyes. He was a trooper; our son is such a strong young man. He powered through very painful hand therapy sessions, and by the end of those appointments, his hand movement was pretty much back to normal. God answered that prayer in a big way!

Next was our follow-up with the neurosurgeon to get the tumor reevaluated on his spine. The tumor was actually causing our son pain, but the shoulder injury had masked the back pain. He had mentioned his back hurting to me, but I brushed it off thinking it was from his fall. The doctor discussed the options with us; we could leave the tumor alone and watch it or have surgery to remove it. My husband and I had already prayed about it, and we wanted that thing out of his body! There was no way the doctor could know what it really was unless they took it out. Our son agreed; it was causing him pain and he wanted it out too.

At the same time, my husband was also facing another big spine surgery. My husband's surgery was already scheduled. My mother-in-law was having hip replacement two weeks *before* my husband's surgery, and my son's back surgery was scheduled three weeks *after* my husband's surgery. I was scheduling my nervous breakdown soon after!

I was seriously having a hard time, but there was nowhere to stop and catch my breath. My family needed me; I had to lean into God for strength every day. The next few months were a complete blur.

My mother-in-law's surgery was first, and it went well. Next up was my husband's middle back surgery, and it was by far the biggest and most painful surgery to date. That says a lot! He was back in ICU for three days and then transferred to a regular room.

A day or so after his surgery, my mother-in-law developed blood clots in her lungs and was rushed to the same hospital where my husband was. You cannot make this stuff up people! She was even on the same floor as my husband, and we could look out our windows and wave at each other. My sister-in-law took care of her while I was taking care of my husband. It was crazy; we had to laugh so we didn't cry.

This surgery took my husband back to ground zero. His incision was eighteen inches long and started at the base of his skull and went all the way down to the bottom of his rib cage. The size of his incision was insane. We had to have some help at home again because he required around-the-clock care. We could not afford to hire a nurse, so family and a few close friends stepped in to stay with my husband when I needed to go to the office or leave the house.

As bad as it may sound, I enjoyed the days that I was in the office. It was the place that I could go and forget my problems at home and have some semblance of normal. I craved normal. I was exhausted but still going one hundred miles an hour trying to keep up with work, home, taking care of kids, and being my husband's round-the-clock caretaker.

Three weeks after my husband's surgery, our youngest son was wheeled into his surgery to remove the tumor on his lumbar spine. Thankfully the surgery went as expected, and the biopsy results were benign. Let me shout *Praise Jesus*! My son had a big long incision on his low back and lots of pain, but that thing was out of his body! They had removed a big portion of the vertebrae, so the healing would take a few months.

My son was able to go home after a few days, and I was thankful to have all my patients back under one roof. Mama was tired. I can't even explain how exhausted I was. Not so much physically, but emotionally I was worn out. I felt like I lived on high alert, constantly waiting for the next shoe to drop, and it was beginning to take its toll on me.

I want to take a quick second to brag on our oldest son. He was a total trooper through all of this. He was a huge help to his dad and brother and lent a hand to help me stay sane. Though he was going to college and working, he always made time to help us out when we needed him. Thank you, sweet boy, for putting your family first. You could have been out doing a million other teenage things, but you stepped up at a time when we needed you most.

Our youngest son's strength inspires me; like his dad, he rarely complains. I will never fully understand the extent of his suffering. It goes without saying, my husband is my hero. He has suffered enough for two lifetimes but never gives up. Most of all, God was with us through it all. I am grateful that He showed up huge when we needed Him the most. I cannot express enough gratitude for a clean report on the tumor taken out of our son's spine.

I often wonder if the stomach virus that landed us in the hospital was God's way of bringing this to light. I was so busy taking care of everybody and everything; I think God had to literally stop me in my tracks and shine it in bright neon lights to get my attention. He kept me stable when once again, I should have been curled up in the fetal position trying to manage a sick husband and a sick child. It was rough, but I always had a place to take my worries, fears, and concerns. God will provide just what you need, when you need it! He proved that time and time again to our family.

Hebrews 4:16

"Let us therefore come boldly unto the throne of grace, that we may obtain mercy, and find grace to help in time of need."

Counting it All Joy

Chapter 4

A SLICE OF HUMBLE PIE

The remainder of 2016 was spent taking care of my patients. We rang in 2017 with high hopes that *surely* this would be the year that things would get better. We all felt like we were due a break. The medical bills that were incurred over the last three years would make a grown man cry. Eight surgeries between my husband and two kids added up quickly.

I was the only one working now, and though my husband's disability check was helpful, most of it went to pay for his insurance premiums and medicine with very little left over. I want to go back to the beginning of our story and share how God provided when the rug was jerked out from under us financially.

When my husband was no longer working and facing multiple surgeries, I prayed constantly for God to make provisions. The medical bills were stacked up and there were more bills than money, and on top of that, our savings were wiped out. My husband mentioned to me one day that maybe we should consider filing bankruptcy so we would not lose everything.

The thought of bankruptcy in and of itself infuriated me. I fought him on this subject tooth and nail for weeks. I would stay up at night with our budget and a calculator trying to figure out a way to avoid filing bankruptcy. I cried, I prayed, I begged, I cried some more, but I ended up conceding and agreed to visit a bankruptcy lawyer.

I cringed at the thought of completely destroying all that we had worked so hard for all these years. My husband was only a few weeks off his first neck-surgery-gone-wrong when we visited the bankruptcy lawyer and was barely able to function. As he sat in a chair with his head propped up on a pillow fighting back tears of pain, I was fighting back tears of embarrassment and humiliation.

How did our lives get completely turned upside down overnight to find us sitting at a bankruptcy lawyer's office? I felt like I was literally dying on the inside and somebody had punched me in the gut. I was *not* on board in the least.

Sometimes prayers get answered in unconventional ways. Bankruptcy would actually turn out to be an answer to a prayer though not as I had expected or planned. I fought back the tears as I explained our situation to the lawyer. He asked a few questions and then gave us his opinion. Though we had randomly picked this lawyer out of the yellow pages like playing a game of pin the tail on the donkey, he turned out to be very kind and helpful.

The lawyer informed us that our best bet would be to file. We would be required to file Chapter 13 due to our income prior to my husband becoming disabled. That meant we would pay back 100% over the next five years. Knowing that I was paying it back made me feel a tad better.

I expressed my concerns about our credit score, but honestly, I didn't see that we had any other options. If we didn't do something, our credit would be destroyed anyway. The lawyer explained that once it was approved, we would make our payments to the trustee each month until it was paid in full.

We had to show up to a court hearing, which was the equivalent of sitting in a room with a bunch of other people, taking our turn at the lawyer table and signing the official papers. I was a complete wreck as I gathered years and years of bank statements and bills. I had to fill out numerous forms and answer a million questions about our finances. But the day I walked out of bankruptcy court, I felt like someone had just lifted the entire world off my shoulders. I could breathe again. I had a plan and that eased the burden.

Fast forward four years, after making payments and adding in extra money like tax refunds, we paid off the bankruptcy almost a year early. Believe it or not, our credit score was not demolished after the bankruptcy was dismissed. The lawyer explained that making all those on-time payments really helped. Our credit score is not perfect now, but it is very good.

Bankruptcy was a blessing. Never thought I would say that in a million years. I am not going to lie, it was tough. We did without a lot of things during those four years. We still drive older, paid for vehicles, and we haven't taken a family vacation in years. Guess what? We survived. What I feared would be the end of us financially was actually a fresh start.

We currently only owe on our house and a few medical bills that came about after the bankruptcy, and then we are debt free. I am proud of that! God saw us through, and I am so grateful. Sometimes what doesn't kill you really does make you stronger.

Our kids also learned some hard but valuable lessons about money too. Our oldest son was graduating high school during the heat of my husband's surgeries and sickness. He got a job when he turned sixteen and saved up and bought his own vehicle. After graduation, he decided to go to the community college to save money.

Our oldest worked hard, sometimes picking up side jobs, to help pay his college tuition and was able to graduate from college debt free. His work ethic is strong, and he makes us proud every day. He is married now with a family of his own, and he is a great provider.

I am not so sure the outcome would have been the same if this had not happened to our family. My husband and I were pretty good at spoiling our kids. We learned so much about our finances and how to live on less. Good can come out of a really crappy situation (that you originally thought would be the end of you) when you surrender your problems to God.

I struggled for a long time over filing for bankruptcy. It looked and felt like failure to me. Yet at the same time, I was truly thankful that it was an option. It was a huge weight off our shoulders, and it wasn't the end of the world like I originally thought it would be. Do I walk around encouraging others to file for bankruptcy? Absolutely not! But I can tell you this, if life hits you so hard that it becomes your only choice, there is life after bankruptcy. And that is why I am sharing this story, to give you hope.

I was so devastated initially and thought our lives were ruined forever; it felt like we were wearing the scarlet letter. We would have probably lost our house and everything we had if we hadn't gone through with the bankruptcy. Dave Ramsey might read that and cringe, but for our family, it worked out in our favor. We came out on the other side with a new realization that we can live cash-only; I say that is a win, and I think Dave would approve.

I went kicking and screaming to the lawyer's office that day, and without even flinching, I admit it was because of my pride. It was humiliating to have to lay it all out on the table. It was definitely a big slice of humble pie that I chowed down on that day. Sometimes we have to do the very thing that we swore we would never do and swallow our pride to do it. When it is all over with, we realize that there were huge lessons to be learned throughout the process, and it was actually a blessing.

I learned how to be smarter with our money; I learned that we wasted a lot of money. My kids learned that money doesn't grow on trees, and if they want something, they can get creative to find a way to earn the money to get it. The experience was a humbling one and so much good came from it. As crazy as it may sound, I thank God that I made it to the bankruptcy lawyer's office that day. In the end, we survived and thrived.

James 4:10

"Humble yourselves in the sight of the Lord, and he shall lift you up."

Chapter 5

THE PRAYER QUILT

After my husband's first surgery in 2014, I was struggling with *everything*. My world felt like it was falling apart, but I had to keep it together for my kids and even my husband. The few times that I broke down in front of them, it upset my kids so bad that I felt guilty for letting my guard down. One night laying in bed, I said out loud that if I didn't have kids, I wished that I could just disappear. My husband didn't even gasp or argue with me. He simply said, "Me too." We were both at the bottom of the slimy pit of despair.

It wasn't that I didn't want to live anymore; I just didn't want to live like *this* anymore. I was tired and depressed; you might say that I was over it! I had prayed so diligently for help, and it seemed like the harder I prayed, the worse our situation got.

I didn't blame God for anything that had happened to our family, but it sure felt like He wasn't listening. I went through a season of feeling very forsaken. Scripture tells me that it is impossible because Jesus promised to never leave us or forsake us, but when you go through a season of feeling like God is silent; it can sure feel that way. I admit my faith was being shaken to the point that I was crumbling.

We both lay in bed that night and cried. We held each other, and I bawled like a baby. There were so many things that were simply out of our control. When your friends start comparing all the hard stuff happening in your life to the book of Job, well, you know it is bad. We both knew it could always be worse, but it was hard to see how anything good could come from all of the pain we felt.

When things get super bad, your gratitude list becomes the basics like, I have a roof over my head, my children are saved and healthy, and my bills got paid this month. We knew we were so blessed, yet life was pelting us left and right and had literally knocked the wind out of us both. We were about as low as you could go, and on this particular night, I wanted to disappear.

I woke up the next morning and moped around the house for a while doing Saturday chores. I heard a knock on the front door, so I went to answer it. There was a little old lady standing on my porch, and I had no idea who she was. I answered the door, and she asked if she had the right house.

What she said next still gives me chills. The lady said, "Honey, I have been driving around for weeks with a prayer quilt in my van for your husband, and I kept meaning to come by but didn't." She went on to tell me that she decided when she woke up this morning that she simply *had* to get this quilt to our family. I stood there with my mouth hanging open. I knew why she was standing on my front porch; God sent her.

Some churches in our town make prayer quilts for people in the community that are sick or going through a hard time. I assume that someone in the church knew of my husband's situation and decided to put him on the prayer quilt list. Before they bring the quilt to the person, they hang it up on a wall in the church, and members of the church tie the strings on the quilt in a knot and say a prayer for the person the quilt is going to. This little lady went on to tell me that so many people had been praying for my husband, and then she added, "And you too honey." Ugly cry happening at this point.

I was speechless. What *timing*! My husband and I had been so low the night before that we both wanted to disappear from this life. We were at our breaking point, and God knew it. I believe with all my heart that God sent this woman to our house. It was not a coincidence that she had *decided* to *finally* stop by. God knew that we needed a firm reminder that He had not forgotten us.

I invited the sweet little lady in, and she went to our bedroom and told my husband about the quilt. As she laid the quilt over him, she showed him all the knots on the quilt that represented prayers that went up for him. She said she sure hoped that he could feel them all. I didn't know about him, but I can tell you that I sure did.

As the lady was leaving, I walked her to the front porch and gave her a big hug. I thanked her for following the Lord to bring us the quilt that day. She had *no* idea how badly we needed the encouragement, and we were so appreciative. So many times when you get to the end of your rope, God will send you a life raft, or maybe even a prayer quilt.

All our problems were not suddenly solved, but God sent us a very strong reminder that day that He had not gone anywhere. Even though we can feel forgotten or forsaken at times, we know it is just the enemy getting into our head telling us lies. We needed a strong reminder.

Later that evening, I asked my husband if I could hold the quilt. l sat down and wrapped the quilt around me. I ran my hands over all of the knots on the quilt that represented prayers, and I thanked God for this very clear sign. I needed it. My husband needed it. I also told the Lord that I was so sorry for letting my problems get me to the point of wanting to throw in the towel. But God had just thrown the towel right back in the form of a prayer quilt.

A few months later, a friend from another church in town showed up at our house with another, you won't believe this, *prayer quilt*! How blessed we are! I cherish them both and what they represent. I will never forget the sweet little lady showing up on our doorstep on a Saturday morning with hope for our family and a message from God to not give up.

2 Timothy 1:7

"For God hath not given us the spirit of fear; but of power, and of love, and of a sound mind."

Chapter 6

MAILBOX MONEY

During the first year of my husband becoming disabled, our finances took a huge hit. Prior to my husband getting sick, we had lived a very comfortable life. Nothing flashy, but we paid the bills, went on vacations, and if we wanted something, we bought it. We always tried to be giving and generous to others less fortunate than we were. We knew we were extremely blessed.

Everything changed when my husband became disabled. We were suddenly living on one income, and the lack of money didn't stop the medical bills from pouring in every day. Multiple surgeries plus doctor visits, medication, home health, physical therapy, and hospital stays added up. Let's just say that most of the time there was way more month than money.

Life was beyond stressful! We filed for my husband's disability as soon as we could, but it can take months and sometimes even years to get approved. I would lie in bed at night pouring over our budget trying to make the numbers work. I felt like I was in the deep end, on my tippy toes, with water up to my nostrils.

Back when I was still in college, unmarried and living at home, my older sister told me about hard times that she and my brother-in-law had gone through as a young couple. When her husband was in school and they were living off his paper route salary, they used to frequently get what she called *mailbox money*.

Money was extremely tight and many months it looked like there wouldn't be enough to cover all the bills. They always prayed for God to make provisions during these tough times and trusted that He would. She shared with me that often money would show up *unexpectedly*, sometimes even the exact amount they needed to pay their bills.

I was young and unconcerned about paying bills at the time, but I never forgot her sharing that story with me. God knew, even way back then, I would need that story later in my life. I never dreamed that someday I would receive my own mailbox money.

Just a few days after my husband's surgery-gone-wrong, we started getting tons of cards in the mail with notes of encouragement and prayers for my husband. Guess what else? Yep, you got it, mailbox money. People would comment in the cards that they felt led to send help to our family.

Every time we would open a card and money would fall out, my husband and I would feel overwhelmed with gratitude. We were so thankful for the help; we could not believe that so many people were thinking about our family.

There were several churches that also sent us love offerings. I don't know if I can even accurately pen down how humbling it was to receive these gifts. It came during our hardest season when life was completely turned upside down. I had cried to the Lord so many nights, begging him to send us help, and it never failed that we would receive just the amount we needed to take care of our needs.

I realized during that season that it is easier to give than receive. My husband and I had always been very generous and never thought twice about helping someone in need. We never expected anything in return. I never dreamed in a million years that someday our family would be on the receiving end. Never!

I struggled tremendously with it all in the beginning as did my husband. We both felt so unworthy, but we learned some very valuable lessons during this time of sparsity. When praying for help, whether it is financial help, encouragement, guidance, support, whatever the case may be, so many times that help comes in the form of people. We are the hands and feet of Jesus, and when the Lord lays it on our hearts to help someone, we just might be the answer to someone's desperate prayers. I often think of that now when I hear that someone needs help, when the Lord lays it on me to help, I do not hesitate. I know without a doubt that God is working on the other end.

The cards in the mail continued for months and months. We were so humbled and blessed by what others were doing for us. Many delicious meals were dropped off at our house as well. Our oldest son worked at Lowes at the time and would come home from work with money or gift cards that people had given him to bring home to his dad.

My husband was unable to go to church during this time, but the boys and I would go every Sunday. We have a Christian handshake at the end of the service, and Sunday after Sunday, I would shake someone's hand and they would slide money into my hand. It would always catch me off guard. I would sit in my car after service or while driving home overwhelmed with gratitude and humility.

Our family *never* asked anyone for help, except God. Week after week people were giving us the help that the Lord knew we needed. I told my mother-in-law one day that I felt so bad because I wasn't sure we would ever be able to pay all these people back. That was definitely my pride speaking. My mother-in-law put it all in perspective for me when she told me to accept the help with gratitude knowing it was coming from God.

I wanted to write this chapter because the mailbox money humbled me to the core of who I am as a human being. My husband would cry when I would read the kind cards out loud to him. We felt so unworthy to even call upon the name of the Lord, but we needed Him every single minute of every single day. He never let us down.

When we didn't have enough money in the bank to pay our bills, mailbox money started showing up. When our vehicles needed repairs but it wasn't in the budget, a church member or friend would *show up* with a love offering taken up for our family, and we would have enough to pay for the repairs. When the medical bills were overflowing and our budget could not stretch to pay them, help would show up out of the blue.

I want to share this with you because I want you to see that even in times of despair, when your world is falling apart, when you cannot see the light of day, God is *there* to *meet* you in your mess. God may not stop the storm or change your circumstances, but He will always send you what you need. Go back and read that sentence again.

Eight years later, my mind is still blown. During that first year when we were dealing with disabilities, lost wages, bankruptcy, pain, suffering, mental exhaustion, humiliation, and despair, God became tangible to us in a way that we had never experienced before. I felt His presence; I saw His hand move on more than one occasion in such a mighty way that it took my breath away.

I suppose the doubters are saying, "If God is so big, then why didn't He heal your husband?" I don't have the answer to that question. I pray every day for healing and restoration, and I believe that God is more than able to heal my husband's broken body. I have learned to trust that if it is the Lord's will, then we will see that prayer answered.

Yet, I also know that sometimes our healing doesn't come as we think it should. The answers to our prayers do not always look like what we expect them to look like.

I firmly believe God did answer our prayers. My husband is still with us, he could have easily died during a surgery or the terrible infection could have killed him. God answered our prayers when he gave us strength for another day. He allowed pain and suffering, but He sent help when we needed it most.

My husband and I are both saved and heaven bound. We both have a better place to go when our time comes. We did pray for God to take away the disabilities, but we don't lose our faith that those prayers have not been answered yet. Even if they are never answered on this side of eternity, we believe that God is good.

We can turn to the scriptures and see that the Apostle Paul had a sickness or injury that he asked the Lord three times to remove from him. A familiar scripture comes right after that (2 Corinthians 12:9–10).

> *"And he said unto me, My grace is sufficient for thee: for my strength is made perfect in weakness. Most gladly therefore will I rather glory in my infirmities, that the power of Christ may rest upon me.*
>
> *Therefore I take pleasure in infirmities, in reproaches, in necessities, in persecutions, in distresses for Christ's sake: for when I am weak, then am I strong."*

I have read those scriptures and heard them preached so many times. When my husband became disabled and I wondered if God would heal his body, these scriptures were my answer. God's grace is all we need. It is *more* than sufficient. When we are weak in our flesh, God is strong. God is able to display His strength in us when we surrender our life to Him and allow Him to be our "everything."

In verse 10, Paul says he takes "pleasure" in infirmities and all the hard stuff he went through. Let me tell you, as crazy as it sounds, I found out exactly what he meant when we were at rock bottom. God's love and grace is so big, so great, and so strong that you will be able to praise Him during the storms of life *even if* He doesn't answer your prayer the way you wanted. *Even if* God doesn't remove the "thorn in the flesh," you can still sing his praises. God felt so close during our weakest and lowest point. When you can shout the praises of God from your wheelchair or hospital bed, you are heading in the right direction. God is good even when life is hard.

Ephesians 3:20

"Now unto him that is able to do exceeding abundantly above all that we ask or think, according to the power that worketh in us."

Counting it All Joy

Chapter 7

A BLESSING IN THE STORM

We closed out 2016 with just a farewell and zero expectations of what 2017 might bring. I had stopped making New Year's resolutions by this point. I continued to pray for the Lord to watch over our family as I tried to keep my eyes on God and off the storm. This would be the first year of no surgeries for my husband, though our youngest son would keep the hospitals in business with two surgeries for a new illness.

Our oldest son was in the last semester of college before he applied for his career program, and our youngest was a junior in high school. Things were still tough, but we all were adjusting to our new normal. I felt like the chaos coordinator of our crazy life.

Raising our boys in church was truly a blessing for me. The Lord saved both boys at young ages, and we were so grateful for that. One was saved on the altar at church and the other in his bed. Both had joined the church soon after they got saved and enjoyed going to church each Sunday.

We had always taught our kids the biblical principles you expect Christian parents to teach their kids, and our boys for the most part seem to adhere to those teachings. Nobody is perfect of course, but you hope that what they are hearing and seeing is sinking in and that they will apply it to their life.

In early spring of 2017, my oldest son and his girlfriend found out they were expecting a child. My son was terrified to tell us as you can only imagine. On a day when I was working from home, he finally mustered up the courage to tell his dad first. My husband, though shocked and concerned, responded in love and kindness and in his usual calm demeanor. Next my son had to find the courage to tell me, his very uptight mother.

I happened to walk through the bedroom where they were sitting and my husband asked me if I would sit down for a minute, our son needed to tell me something. I sat down on the edge of the couch and looked over at my son. My heart knew without him even saying a word.

To be completely honest, I didn't handle the news very well, I was very upset. My son was twenty years old, still in college, living at home, working a part time job; how would he be able to take care of a family? We had been through the fire the last few years, how would we be able to take on anything else? My heart was heavy for him and for his girlfriend. This was going to definitely change their future plans, and I knew it would force them to grow up fast.

I don't think I slept for a week. My heart was completely overwhelmed with worry, anxiety, and yes, I will admit, embarrassment too. I am a preacher's wife; you try so hard to teach your kids and pray you have set a good example. This was definitely not how I had planned our child's future.

After many sleepless nights and going face down in prayer pouring my heart out to God, I felt like the Lord was telling me to let go of my idea of "perfect" and embrace my son right where he was. I had to let go of the fears of what others would think or say and go and wrap my arms around these two terrified kids and love them. My husband handled the news way better than I did; he reminded me often that we were not perfect either and every one of us needs grace.

God is so very good. This baby was an unexpected blessing and a light that shined in our very dark season of life. Fast forward to today, our little granddaughter is our sunshine. We absolutely *adore* her. She has brought so much joy into our world that I cannot imagine our life without her. I have asked God so many times to forgive me for my initial reaction. While I was surprised at the news, God was never caught off guard. When I cried out to Him so many times worried about how this would all work out, He already knew.

Life is full of surprises. Did I want my son to be out of school and married first before he started a family? Absolutely! Could I change what happened? No, I couldn't. I felt the Lord nudging me to let go of the sorrow over the life I had so carefully planned out for my kids and trust that it would all work out and be okay.

Nobody is perfect, and I have been guilty of going to great lengths to make our life appear pretty perfect on the outside by only showing the world our dressed up highlight reel. What is kind of funny is that anyone that knew us at all knew that our life was far from problem free. Who did I think I was fooling? We still hold on to our biblical principles and beliefs, but that doesn't mean that things will always go according to our well-intentioned plans.

I had so much going on in my life already; I was literally hanging on by a thread. When this news came along, it was *almost* the straw that broke the camel's back. It was *almost* the thing that broke me. I had been through one thing after another year after year with no break. Admitting that was hard and it took some time for me to adjust to the news.

I sat one afternoon with my stepmom, pouring out my heart to her and riding the struggle bus. She gave some wonderful advice that day by telling me to let go of the perfect life I had planned for my son and embrace him and love him right where he was. He needed my love not my chastisement. She spoke truth to me, and I needed to hear it.

I was forty-eight years old, and people teasing me and calling me "grandma" felt so odd in the beginning. I finally settled on a "grandma" name that I felt suited me, and I began to open my heart to the idea of becoming a grandparent. It was an awkward feeling at first, but just like all the other changes that had come barreling into our lives, I began to get excited to meet this baby girl.

I would look at my son at times and could still see the little boy that would sit on my lap and want me to read him a book. Then I would look at him and see him for the man that he had become. I was very proud that he was stepping up to the plate to become a dad. I was in awe of how hard he was working to provide for his soon-to-be family.

Chapter 7: A Blessing in the Storm

Letting go of my baby when it was time for him to grow up and be on his own was tough for me. My children are my world and my motivation to keep going. I am not really sure where I would be if I hadn't had my kids to keep me grounded and focused when our world was crashing down around us.

On days when I wanted to stay in the bed and pull the covers up over my head, I couldn't. I had two boys that were depending on me to get up and not quit. They still needed me, but in a little different way, and I did not want to disappoint. I was also gaining a "daughter," and I wanted her to feel nothing but love from me.

My oldest brother came to me after my son told him the news and gave me a big bear hug. I wasn't sure what his reaction was going to be, but with tears in his eyes, he assured me that this baby would be one of the best things that would ever happen to us. He told me to get excited and ready for my heart to explode with love. I think back on that conversation many times and I smile.

My experience in this chapter was a humbling one. I wanted to feel some semblance of control in my life, and I think I became somewhat controlling when it came to my boys and what they were doing or how we were perceived. My life felt like a train wreck, but I had worked super hard at doing all the "right" things for my kids and had big expectations for their lives. I didn't leave much room for them to be human.

I learned so much from this experience. God used it to draw me closer to Him and to help me relinquish the imaginary control that I "thought" I had over my life and even my kids' lives. The only thing we can really control in this life is our own attitude and how we respond when faced with challenges.

We can be good parents and raise our kids in church and teach them right from wrong. We can discipline our kids and train them to be good moral human beings. Once they get older and out from underneath our wings, they are on their own to make decisions. Some will make you proud and some might make you cringe. Some will make you smile and some will make you cry. But at the end of the day, no matter what, you love them more than life itself, and even better, God loves them most of all.

I found a wooden sign one day at Hobby Lobby that says "There is a blessing in the storm," and I feel like that might be our family motto. The devil comes to kill, steal, and destroy whatever he can get his hands on. We can fight against the devil with the word of God and prayer. We can look at the storms of life and only see the bad that the storms bring, or we can look for the positives and the beautiful rainbow after the storm.

God is with us in the storm, and He can turn hurt and pain into beautiful things if we let Him. We must let go of our plans and let God be the architect of our life and our children's lives. His ways are definitely higher than our ways, and they are always perfect. I am so thankful for His perfect plans for my life, they are so much better than anything I could have dreamed up. God is always good.

I have spent a lot of time on my knees in prayer asking God to forgive me for many things. I didn't react very well to the news my son gave us that day. I know it had to be the hardest thing he has ever done in his life. To come to his devout Christian parents and share the news that he was going to be a dad as a twenty year old, still living at home, still in school and unmarried, was probably one of the hardest things he has ever done.

My daughter-in-law and my son chose life for their child. They could have easily taken it a different direction out of fear of how their news would be received. They were brave and took ownership. I am beyond proud of *both* of them and how they have handled it all. They are wonderful parents, and I am so thankful for them and the beautiful, sweet life that we all adore and love so much.

I pray my granddaughter will always know how much she is loved and more importantly, that God loves her even more. My biggest prayer for her life is that she will someday find the Lord precious to her soul. I pray my son gives her the same opportunities he was given to hear the truth about how to be saved. Whether I am here to see it or not, that is my every day prayer for her. She was the blessing in our storm. She was everything I never knew I always wanted.

Hebrews 11:1

"Now faith is the substance of things hoped for, the evidence of things not seen."

Counting it All Joy

Chapter 8

A HARD GOODBYE

2017 had its challenges for sure, but it also came with a few big blessings. My oldest son was accepted into his career program at school, something that he worked so hard to get into. With a baby on the way, we felt like he was taking steps in the right direction for his future. When my son called one day to tell me he had been selected for his program, I had to sit down and catch my breath and thank God for an answered prayer.

We were so proud of our son and could see the Lord was working in his life. A baby on the way helped him earn a grant that would cover almost 100% of his tuition his final year. Up until this point, he had been working and paying his own way. It was such a relief and a blessing to have that last year paid for. This enabled him to concentrate on saving his money for the new arrival. Another answered prayer!

Our youngest son was still having some health issues; he ended up having two surgeries towards the end of 2017. There were so many days that I felt we could not win for losing. We would take two steps forward and three steps backwards with his health. We spent a lot of time that year at the children's hospital trying to figure out what was going on with him. Having a sick child that we could not find the answers for was wearing us all down.

After much prayer, our son was finally referred to a specialist that I truly believe was godsent. He became more than a doctor to us; he treated us like family and took a special interest in helping our son overcome his health issues. My son had been sick for so long at this point, he was in and out of school, having to be taught at home, I cried out to God daily for relief and answers. This doctor was the help we had been searching for, and he got our son going in the right direction to healing.

Our youngest son is now nineteen years old and has regained his health for the most part over the course of two very long and very worrisome years. It didn't come in one fell swoop, it was little by little, baby stepping his way back to health. Sometimes I just have to stop what I am doing, look at my son, and remember how far we have come. Thank you, Jesus, for watching over him, caring for him, and giving him back the gift of his health.

We were closing out the year with gratitude for a new grandbaby, for a new daughter-in-law, and for a feeling of joy. Nothing could have ever prepared me for what was coming next.

At the beginning of November, our granddaughter made her grand entrance into our lives. She was absolutely precious. She was a beautiful mixture of both her parents and soon had all of us wrapped around her little finger. The love and joy that this tiny little human brought into all of our lives was intense. My husband and I were completely in love with this sweet little surprise. I realized that God knew exactly what we

Chapter 8: A Hard Goodbye

needed and when we needed it. Our baby girl would be the bright spot in our lives for the dark days ahead.

Christmas that year was full of excitement. We were new grandparents excited to spoil our little granddaughter. The boys and I spent the Saturday before Christmas at my dad's house celebrating with that side of the family. It was a great day of food and lots of fellowship and laughter. We had taken fun family pictures and enjoyed our day together. Everyone took turns holding our new grandbaby, and happiness was in the air.

Two days later, we held my mom's Christmas celebration at my house. Everyone on that side of the family was excited to meet our granddaughter also. My oldest brother was one of the last ones to leave my house that night, and as I walked him to the door to tell him goodbye, I gave him a quick side hug and said, "I love ya!"

Nothing could have prepared me for the frantic phone call that I would receive two days later from his wife. My brother had collapsed and was in the ambulance on his way to the hospital. Thankfully, I was working at the office that day about five minutes away.

My sister-in-law told me that my brother appeared to have had a stroke, but the CT scan at the ER showed he had a mass on his brain so he was being transferred to a trauma hospital. She was also on her way to the hospital but was stuck in traffic. She was not having any luck getting my parents to answer their phone, and she asked me to try getting a hold of them. My world just stopped.

I immediately tried calling both my parents and kept getting their voicemail. I hated to do it but I sent them a group text telling them to call me immediately. Not the text you want to get from your kid. My phone rang about a minute later, and my mom was hysterical; she had no idea what was wrong, but knew something bad must have happened. She wept as I told her the news about my brother. I left work hurriedly and drove straight to the hospital.

I arrived at the hospital before the ambulance and anyone else, so I stood outside on the sidewalk waiting and praying. I was a complete wreck. I could hear sirens and could see the ambulance coming down the street. I was literally begging God to please help my brother.

They backed the ambulance into the parking spot outside the ER, and I felt completely weak in the knees. I told the ambulance drivers that the patient was my brother as they were unloading him. My brother was still conscious but seemed very confused as his eyes darted back and forth in the sunlight. I could not imagine how scared he was. I touched his cheek and told him I loved him and that it was going to be okay. They had to get him inside quickly, so I stood on the sidewalk outside the ER silently begging God for my brother's life.

A short while later, I was allowed to go to my brother's ER room to see him. He was still conscious but not able to respond much at all. The doctor's told us his condition was critical and they needed to put him into an induced coma to try and stop the brain bleed. I held my brother's hand and told him I loved him again, unsure if he could really hear me. This would be the last time I would see him truly awake. *Ever.*

My parents got to the hospital a short time later, and soon the waiting room was a flurry of family and friends hearing the news and coming to check on us.

Chapter 8: A Hard Goodbye

We were not given much hope, but we came together as a family as we sat in the ashes and waited for news on my brother's condition. This became our new normal for the next ten days.

I stayed at the hospital until about 2:00 a.m. that first night. With my brother in ICU and no visitation till the next morning, I decided to drive home. The Lord and His angels must have guided me home that night because I cried so hard on the way home that I couldn't see the road. I *screamed* prayers and lamented with God to spare my brother's life. I sobbed so hard I could barely breathe.

By the grace of God, I pulled in my driveway and went inside and lay in the bed. It felt surreal that my lifelong partner in crime, my protector, my strong and healthy big brother was lying in a hospital bed fighting for his life. Once again, I felt like life had just punched me in the gut.

We spent New Year's in a hospital waiting room just down the hallway from my brother, still on a ventilator and not giving us too many signs that he was still with us. We greeted 2018 with fervent prayer for him to pull through. Watching my family grieve this tragedy was almost more than I could bear. We were all trying to be positive and hold it together for each other. My niece and nephew were hanging on to hope that their dad would pull through; it was devastating.

After a long ten days, my sister-in-law decided to turn off my brother's life support. It is so hard to let someone go, even when you know it is for the best. My brother would not have wanted to linger in a coma-like state. When his life support was turned off, we all gathered around my brother's bedside to be with him as he left this world. The hospital lifted the strict restrictions, and we were all allowed in his room. We loved on him; we sang to him, we prayed over him, we talked to him, and we gave him permission to let go and journey to his heavenly home.

My brother lived for almost eleven hours after his life support was turned off. I was at the end of his bed, holding on to his foot, as I watched him take his last breath. He passed peacefully at 12:55 a.m. on January 8, 2018, surrounded by family. A piece of my heart went with him.

Grief is so strange. I cried so many tears during my brother's hospital stay that when it came time for his funeral, I was honestly all cried out. I felt numb and couldn't shed another tear. My mind went back to my memories and the recent time I had spent with my brother. We had *just* spent Christmas together; I had *just* hugged him and told him I loved him; we had *just* stood in my kitchen and talked about his full work schedule. We had *just* talked on the phone for over an hour two days before. It didn't seem real that he was gone. I still catch myself thinking that I need to ask him a question, and then the reality hits me that I can't—he is gone.

Watching my family grieve his death has been heartbreaking. I had to give myself permission to grieve my brother's death. Being a "caretaker" for the last several years, I held in so many of my emotions so I would not upset my family.

During this time, I allowed myself to grieve. Maybe that will make sense to someone in my shoes. We try so hard to appear strong and stoic because we don't want to upset the apple cart, but after my brother's death, I gave myself permission to flip the apple cart if it made me feel better.

Chapter 8: A Hard Goodbye

It was a hard goodbye. I don't question God as to why it happened and why him. I know those are questions that we won't get answers to. I try and cherish the time I had with my brother. I have finally reached a place that I can tell my "Jeff stories" and smile at the fun memories. I still have days where it will hit me out of nowhere that he is gone, and I have to have a good cleansing cry. Those days of crying are fewer and farther between now. Yet grief will hit you out of nowhere sometimes and you feel like it just happened.

God felt so close to me during my brother's illness and death. He was there for me during those late nights as I was driving home from the hospital. He was there when my brother took his last breath. He was there when we closed the casket for the last time. He was real and tangible as we grieved and missed my brother so much. Losing someone you love is devastating, and watching my parents lose a child took my breath. I believe losing a child is the greatest loss we can experience on earth.

I want to give some hope too. Our peace resides in the fact that my brother was saved and ready to meet Jesus. Although he had exciting plans for his life, he was a mover and a shaker and a successful business man, he was not expecting to collapse that day. He had big plans, but God had different plans. It is so important to be ready to meet Jesus because we do not know when that appointment will be.

My brother was not living in fear of that day, he was living and enjoying life, and when that day came, he was prepared. So while death is hard, it is final and it is unknown, when you know the Lord and are prepared to meet Him, you are a winner either way.

Ask yourself this important question, where do you stand with God? If you die today, where are you going?

I urge you to make peace with God now if you haven't. How do you get saved? Salvation comes at the end of a humble prayer of repentance and complete surrender. You must *believe* with all your heart, putting your *complete* trust and faith in Jesus. There is no canned prayer that you can repeat. We must work out our own salvation with fear and trembling. Keep asking and keep seeking Him till you *know* you have found Him. It is a heart work, not head knowledge.

How will you know? The trouble disappears and sweet peace comes into your heart. Salvation is our greatest gift; it is our ticket to heaven. The Lord saved my soul when I was sixteen years old. I heard my best friend give her testimony at school, and the trouble hit me like a ton of bricks. I knew I didn't have what she had. I went for a few weeks till I couldn't take it anymore. I fell to my knees on a cold Thursday night in January, and I begged the Lord to save me and give me peace. I remember asking Him to "help me." When the trouble left and the peace came in, there was no mistaking that something had just happened. I knew I had Jesus in my heart; no one had to tell me.

I pray that you make your altar somewhere on this side of eternity and humble yourself to pray until you know you have it too. My salvation is my greatest gift here on earth. I have not always treated it as I should, but I know without a shadow of a doubt that what the Lord did for me on that Thursday night in 1985 is going to take me to heaven someday. Praise Jesus for saving a wretch like me.

Psalm 30:5

"Weeping may endure for a night but joy cometh in the morning."

Counting it All Joy

Chapter 9

YOU CAN'T POUR FROM AN EMPTY CUP

Self-care was the *last* thing on my mind after my husband became sick. When you become a caretaker, every minute of your day seems to get gobbled up meeting someone else's needs. I was taking care of my husband round the clock. In addition, I was raising two teenage boys and one had a lot of health issues. Working full time while trying to stay on top of everything else kept me going in a million directions. My schedule was jam packed.

To add insult to injury, I was also beginning to go through menopause. There was a storm brewing. I was tired, I wasn't eating right, and though I had good intentions to exercise on my lunch break, I had really let myself go. I didn't mean to. After years of living literally on the edge of my seat waiting for the next ball to drop, it just happened. I would lay in bed at night exhausted but unable to sleep. I had a perpetual to-do list rolling around in my brain. God was going to get my attention in a big way.

It was a typical February day. I was working from home and decided to run an errand on my lunch break. I drove to the store to grab a few things, and when I was getting out of the car, I felt like I was going to pass out. I grabbed my cell phone and called my oldest son and told him I felt very sick and needed him to come take me to the hospital. I really thought I was a goner; I was on the verge of blacking out.

I staggered into the store and the clerk asked me if she needed to call the ambulance. At first I said yes and sat down on the floor and drank a bottle of water. I felt a tiny bit better after the water, so I told her to hold off on the ambulance. Even sitting on the dirty floor of a dollar store, I was in complete denial that I needed help. I slowly walked back to my car to wait for my son and prayed for help. I knew God was telling me to be still, but I am not very good at being still.

I talked to God while I waited, asking him to spare me. I had so many people that depended on me. I could have taken two ambulance rides by the time my oldest son showed up. I don't think he understood that this was an emergency. When he finally got there, I moved to the passenger seat and told him to put the pedal to the metal, mama was sick.

When we arrived at the ER, I was quickly taken to a room, and they started a heart monitor and an IV. My blood pressure was *off* the charts. I was administered medicine to help bring it down and was told to try and relax. Did they know who they were talking to? I was wound up tighter than a ball of yarn. I am not very good at relaxing either.

While I was laying there trying to calm down, in comes my younger son into my ER room pushing my husband in his wheelchair. To make matters worse, my husband had called my entire family, and I was not happy about it. I was upset because I didn't want anyone worrying about me, especially my parents. I kind of let my husband have it for calling the whole world. I was silently asking myself why I was so upset. My husband was worried sick; he knew my parents would want to know that their daughter was at the hospital. Yet, I was still not happy about it.

The longer I lay there, the more irritated I got. I kept asking the nurse when I could go home. I told her that I was only on my lunch break and needed to get back home to check emails. Everyone in the room was looking at me like I was a crazy woman. The nurse looked at my husband and then over to me and told me to sit tight. They were running blood work and checking my heart enzymes, I would be there for a while.

Laying on the gurney in the ER that day, I realized that I had been giving and giving but had totally ignored my own health and warning signs. It was like God was telling me if I was not going to take time for myself on my own, He was going to force me to do it the hard way. The crazy train had been running full steam on the track for way too long, it was time to slow down a minute and reevaluate. I had to start making time for myself or I wasn't going to be around to take care of everyone else. I had a big fat wakeup call that day.

The ER doctor was not amused with my attitude. He asked me why I didn't call 911 when I felt like I was going to black out. I told him that I was in denial. Yep, I did. I was half kidding, half serious. He started going over my results and told me that my heart enzymes were all normal so I had not had a heart attack. Wait. What?

It was starting to sink in now. Next the doctor asked me if I had a lot of stress in my life. I paused a minute, looked over at my husband sitting in his wheelchair and then back to the doctor, and chuckled a little. Seriously, how do you explain the last few years in a yes or no answer? I finally answered that I definitely had high stress and I knew I needed to start taking better care of myself.

My blood pressure came back down to normal after a few hours, and I was finally sent home with a prescription for blood pressure pills and told to follow up with my family doctor. The whole episode scared my husband to death. And it did me too when I really stopped to think about what could have happened that day. I took the next day off from work and tried to get a plan together to start making time for myself. I knew things had to change or I wasn't going to be around to take care of my family. It felt like God was telling me it was time to take care of myself and not just everyone else. Easier said than done, but I knew I had to try.

I decided I would give up caffeine and start exercising every day in lieu of taking blood pressure medicine. I was able to get my blood pressure back to a normal range with those two simple changes along with losing a few pounds. After my yearly gynecologist visit a few months later, I also found out that I was starting to go through menopause. Great! Let the fun begin. Talk about change, just about everything in my life had changed and now I was going through "the change."

I was forty-seven years old and was a hot mess. This news explained the brain fog and sleepless nights. I could fall asleep, but I couldn't stay asleep and would lie for hours tossing and turning. Menopause is no joke folks. There are tons of symptoms you can experience and I was having about half of them. I started putting the pieces of the puzzle together, and it made sense why I felt like I had been riding the crazy train to nowhere. Stress seemed to make my symptoms worse.

Chapter 9: You Can't Pour From an Empty Cup

What a wakeup call from God. I had pushed and pushed myself for so long, and now I was paying the price. But God, He was so merciful to me. I prayed for relief, He sent me relief. He was with me as I was being rushed to the hospital, and I seriously thought that was it for me. I am grateful that God spared my life that day. It wasn't my time to go.

I also learned that you cannot pour from an empty cup. If you have flown in an airplane, what are you supposed to do in case of an emergency? We all know, we are supposed to put the oxygen mask on ourselves first so that we can help others. If you don't make time for yourself, you cannot serve others well. When I don't allow myself "me time," I am not very nice to my family. I can be short and grumpy towards them. It is not anything that they have done but that I have not practiced self-care.

I think we have the idea that it is selfish to make ourselves a priority. For several years when my husband was so sick, I did not allow myself any down time. I kept thinking I would do it later, when things slowed down. Okay, you have read the book thus far; you can see that nothing has slowed down for our family. You may be the same. We will always be busy, we will always have something that is demanding our attention, but we must learn self-care and not feel guilty about it.

For me, self-care is nothing elaborate. If I am feeling overloaded, I might jump in the car and go for a long drive, cranking up the music. I might go get lost in TJ Maxx. Even if I don't buy anything, just having some time for myself makes me feel better. Oh, who are we kidding? I don't think I have ever walked out of a TJ Maxx empty-handed.

My point is, take time to do something that fills your cup back up. Go for a walk, read a book, take a bubble bath, get your nails done. Go outside and enjoy nature and get some fresh air. Have lunch with a friend. There is nothing I enjoy any better than taking a day to spend with my best friend. Free therapy folks. I always feel better when I have spent time with her. She helps fill my cup back up. Bible study is also an excellent way to fill up your cup. If you don't know where to start, open up your Bible to Psalms and start reading. I read through the book of Psalms many times over when my husband was so sick. It was balm for my soul.

Find something that makes you happy and sparks joy. When I have done something that puts the pep back in my step, I am definitely a better human being. Remember, it is *not* selfish to practice self-care. I am giving you permission to do something just for you! So go ahead, just do it!

Philippians 4:6–7

"Be careful for nothing; but in every thing by prayer and supplication with thanksgiving let your requests be made known unto God. And the peace of God, which passeth all understanding, shall keep your hearts and minds through Christ Jesus."

Chapter 10

FIND YOUR JOY

I never dreamed I would write a book, but the Lord had different plans. I would wake up in the middle of the night with chapters scrolling through my mind. I lost sleep wrestling with what to do with it.

Parts of my story are, well, *embarrassing*. It sounded absolutely absurd to me that I would somehow be able to sit down and actually write a book. I struggle to even sit down and *read* an entire book.

When I was going through some of the tough times I have shared with you, it never failed that someone would share a part of their story with me and it would help me, encourage me, and give me hope when I was at the end of my rope. Those folks had been through hard stuff too, but they shared their story with me, and it was a huge help. So now I hope that *my* story can help someone realize that there is life in and after the storm, and you can be happy again.

For the first couple of years after my husband became disabled, I barely left the house except to go to work or church. I didn't allow myself a break from being a caretaker, and it really started getting heavy. I even skipped my 30th class reunion because I couldn't picture myself standing around listening to everyone else's success stories when my life felt like a dumpster fire. My best friend didn't even try to change my mind; I think she knew it was too much for me.

After a few years went by, my husband began to encourage me to start doing things without him. He wanted me to get out and see family and friends and have some fun again. I felt guilty at first; it didn't feel right that he wasn't by my side. Eventually I realized that I needed to find some joy again.

So how do you find joy when life has handed you a bowl of sour lemons? I had to find my place in life again that didn't feel so weirdly awkward. Hanging out with other couples without my husband made me feel like the third wheel. My husband is not able to jump in the car and run to the store, he is not able to drive anymore. He can't do any of the outside chores that were his responsibility at one time. I had to learn to let others help me when I needed help. If we refuse help from others, we rob *them* of *their* blessing. Read that again. Accept help friend, it is okay!

I think my biggest path to getting my joy back was a gratitude list. I had to let go of the life that I had so carefully planned for so many years. I had to let go of perfection and accept that even if things never got any better, or God forbid they got worse, my joy doesn't come from my circumstances, it comes from God. I had to dig deep into my faith and know without a shadow of a doubt that when life is devastating, God is still good. I had to come to believe that with all my heart.

I also had to let go of my disappointment and be okay with the hand that we had been dealt. This was a journey; it was not a five-minute decision to be happy again. It took years for me to finally be able to let go of so much that I was carrying deep inside and finally say, "Okay God, I will be content and happy right where I am now. Even if this is as good as it gets, I will find joy again."

I began to allow myself to dream again. For so many years, my mentality was to just survive the day I was in. I didn't look forward and allow myself to have hope. I sat in the ashes drowning in sorrow. I finally realized that my joy didn't come from my circumstances; my joy comes from the Lord. Period. My joy comes from knowing God in the most up close and personal way. If I had not walked through the trials and troubles that came my way, my faith would not have been tested and tried. My relationship with God became strong and intimate through the storm. Our faith will be tried in the fire and shaped into something beautiful.

I gave myself permission to be happy again, even if life was not perfect. I think so many times we keep thinking things will get better so we keep putting off our happiness. What if things stay the same or even get worse? We have to learn to be content in the good seasons and the hard seasons. I realized that I had to choose joy; it wasn't going to just slap me in the face. I had to seek it, I had to cultivate it, and I had to literally make the conscious choice to "choose joy" every single day.

God is the source of our joy. So when we choose Him and find ways to connect and stay connected to Him, the joy comes. When we are disconnected from God and seeking our joy from the world, we fight to find true, heartfelt joy. Yes, there are lots of pleasures in this world that can make us think we are happy, but that happiness seems to fade with time. Learning to be content when your world is falling apart is not easy, but when we turn to God with our heartbreak, we can walk away with the peace that is hard to even understand.

Find your joy. Don't wait for your world to be perfect to decide you can be happy again. Learn to be content in the middle of the storm and not put it off until the storm passes. I did that for a long time, and then I realized that my storm might not ever pass. I decided it was now or never. I allowed myself to be happy right in the middle of the storm.

I hope and I pray that my story helps someone realize that they are not alone in their troubles and sorrow. I hope that it helps someone realize that even when your life plans go belly-up, it doesn't mean it is the end of your story. It might just be a new beginning and a fresh start. I hope my story makes you reach deep into your faith when the storm is knocking you to and fro. I hope my story helps someone realize that God is in the valley as well as on the mountaintop, and joy can even be found deep in the valley. God will meet you there in such a way that when you walk out of the valley, you are not even the same person. I mean that in a good way.

God loves us and He wants us to be happy, but He also wants us to look to Him first and foremost—to allow Him to be our joy. Maybe you are shaking your head no, that doesn't sound like joy to you. You want all the stuff, all the money, a trouble-free life, to heck with all of this walking in the valley stuff. You want the mountaintop. The mountaintop is an amazing place, it truly is. If I ever make it back to the top, I will never take it for granted again. But I want those that are midway down or even face down in the dirt to realize that there are better days ahead, even if they are still hard. Just don't give up. The devil will twist and turn the truth, and we just have to keep looking to God for our truth.

My life is nothing like what I expected it to be, but I have learned to enjoy the simple things with my husband. We enjoy a trip through the drive-through now instead of a sit-down dinner date at a restaurant. We appreciate laying in bed at night watching a movie together. We enjoy our talks and quiet time together so much more than before he became disabled. We appreciate each other more than ever. We know that life can change in the blink of an eye, so we should cherish today.

We live a pretty modest life, and at times when I scroll Facebook and see all the cool stuff others are getting to do with their spouses, it kind of stings. At the same time, I know that I am exactly where God has placed me, and I want Him to get the honor and glory from my life. My life can be simplistic and God still gets the honor and glory. I hope my story helps someone to not give up and to believe in the goodness of God. Let God be the source of your joy.

Psalm 118:24

"This is the day which the Lord hath made; we will rejoice and be glad in it."

Counting it All Joy

Chapter 11

GRATITUDE CHANGES THE ATTITUDE

Having gratitude is a great attitude adjustment. Right after my husband became disabled and life was throwing us curve balls one right after another, I struggled with everything. One day as I was sitting in my office alone feeling sorry for myself, my youngest walked in and saw my tears. He asked me what was wrong, so I told him I was just worried about his dad and it felt like God wasn't listening.

What my son said next is etched in my memory forever, and it snapped me out of the pity party I was having for myself. He said, "Mom! Where's your faith?" He went on to say, "It's like that song we sing at church that says if God takes everything away from us, we can still say that God is good." I gave him a big hug, wiped my tears, and knew that I had to pull myself together. I decided that day to turn my worry into worship. I knew God had heard my prayers and it was time to find something to be grateful for despite our devastating circumstances.

Having a grateful attitude when everything in your life is falling apart is not easy. Yet, when I started focusing on what *was* good in my life and stopped focusing so much on all that was wrong, my whole outlook changed. As I began to let go of all the negativity and began *looking* for things to be thankful for each day, my entire mindset shifted. It slowly became a habit to take a deep breath when something bad or unexpected would happen as I tried looking for the silver lining.

I vividly remember the numerous times we spent in and out of the children's hospital with our youngest son. Walking the halls of a children's hospital will put *everything* in perspective. Over and over again I realized that as bad as our situation was, it could *always* be worse. One day my youngest and I were leaving the hospital after one of his stays and as we were walking down the hallway to the elevator, we passed a grieving mother sitting outside a hospital room sobbing in the arms of several staff members. My son and I stood quietly a few feet away at the elevator waiting for the doors to open. After we stepped in and the doors closed behind us, my son turned to me and said, "I am blessed to be able to walk out of this hospital today. As bad as I have felt this week, I have nothing to complain about." I couldn't have agreed more. Sometimes we need a hard reminder that our problems aren't so terrible when stacked up against someone else's.

When my younger brother and his wife were expecting their first child together several years ago, our entire family was over the moon excited to welcome a new baby into the family. All of our kiddos were grown, so the thought of a new baby to love and spoil was so thrilling! My sister-in-law had a smooth and trouble free pregnancy and our sweet baby girl came into the world a little over five pounds but seemingly healthy. After a few months, it became more and more obvious that something might be wrong as she was not meeting the typical milestones for her age.

My brother and sister-in-law began to raise questions and concerns to their pediatrician, and after a few months, our sweet girl was sent for a MRI of her brain. The results were devastating. Baby girl would face many challenges in life, and it all seemed so completely unfair. I cannot imagine what my brother and sister-in-law were feeling as they stared down the lifelong challenges that would come with raising a child with special needs.

As agonizing as it all was, they picked themselves up, dug deep into their faith, and my brother and sister-in-law became the biggest advocates for their daughter. Family, friends, church family, and even strangers rallied behind them as they started a new and unexpected journey with their daughter.

I watched from the sidelines as my brother and sister-in-law were open and honest about their pain and fears of the unknown. I also saw them find so much joy in raising their precious daughter in the midst of their difficult circumstances. They are the *best* parents, and I admire their faith and strength more than they will ever know. Our sweet girl can *literally* light up a room with her smile. She has made a difference in this world even though she has never spoken a word. God doesn't make mistakes, and while we may never understand why this happened, we can be certain that God will use her story for good and His glory. My niece has brought so much love and joy into the world and no doubt has changed lives.

It may never make total sense why we have to go through some of the things that we do, but trials in our lives can help us grow spiritually and develop a deeper dependence on God. We were never promised an easy life, but we were also never meant to go at it alone. We can find so much hope in the scriptures and plenty of examples of how to walk in faith when our circumstances are less than desirable or even downright heart breaking. If we can take our eyes off our hardships and fix them on Him, the author and finisher of our faith, we can get through anything.

Trials do no come to destroy us, but try telling that to the parent that has lost a child, to the grieving widow, to the young couple that struggle with infertility, or the person that just found out they have a terminal illness. How do you explain that everything will be okay to the parent of a wayward child or to the husband that has lost his job and cannot provide for his family? How do we look at the scripture that tells us to "count it all joy" when we have lost the thing we love most and our suffering is more than we can bear?

Through all the difficulties that my family faced, our faith grew as we turned to God to be our strength when we had none left. We learned to wait on the Lord for answers to our prayers even when the road ahead seemed dark and hopeless at times. We had no choice but to persevere during the trials and put all of our trust in God to bring us through. Waiting on the Lord grew our faith *and* our patience, but there was nothing easy about it.

Honestly, it took me a while to understand how we can "count it all joy" when going through really hard things. It is not in our human nature to look at heartbreak and find joy in it. I finally realized that the trials come to teach us where our help comes from *and* to help us learn to persevere through the hardships. What good comes out of your faith being tried? We develop stronger faith, more patience as we surrender what is out of our control to the Lord, increased trust in God, and most importantly, we realize that our joy comes from God and not our circumstances.

Chapter 11: Gratitude Changes the Attitude

A scripture comes to mind from 1 Peter 4:12–13, *"Beloved, think it not strange concerning the fiery trial which is to try you, as though some strange thing happened to you: But rejoice, inasmuch as ye are partakers of Chris's sufferings; that, when his glory shall be revealed, ye may be glad also with exceeding joy."* In a nutshell, this scripture is reminding us to *not* be surprised when troubles come our way, instead *expect* them! They are all part of our Christian walk as we suffer for Christ's sake. Our hardships do not determine the character of God.

As I have grown and matured in my faith over the years, I have learned to turn to God first when I am in the midst of a fiery trial. I don't even flinch at things now that would have literally taken me over the edge a few years ago. I am able now to look at the trials and ask God what He may be trying to teach me or show me through the troubles. This took years, a lot of tears, many "why me moments," and even some angry fist shaking at God as I cried out to Him in my despair. I definitely don't have all the answers; I can only speak from my own experience. What I can say with zero hesitation is that having gratitude when I wanted to complain helped me get to a place that I could trust God with my hardships and praise Him even when the storms raged all around me.

So how do you begin to practice gratitude? I simply started with a pen and a notebook. I started writing down a list of things I was thankful for every day, even when I didn't feel like it. Over time, my list grew, and I began to look for more things to write in my gratitude journal. Without even realizing it, my attitude completely shifted as I began to focus on what was good in my life and stopped obsessing over what was not. The mere exercise of acknowledging the things I was thankful for made me realize how truly blessed I am.

Did all this gratitude make all my troubles go away? I wish I could say it did, but my circumstances did not change. The hard stuff I was dealing with did not go away, but the way that I viewed it was different. I no longer looked at everything bad that happened to my family as a disaster sent to destroy us. Instead I started asking God what He was trying to teach me and looked to Him for guidance to navigate through the pain and hard places knowing that He would use my pain for His good.

Though I was technically still in the bottom of the pit because my circumstances had not changed, my perception had. I realized that you don't have to have every prayer answered and have everything be perfect to be back on the mountaintop. When you are *spiritually* on the mountaintop with God, it doesn't really matter what your physical situation is. You can feel joy right in the middle of your mess. When you surrender your heartbreak to God and have a heart that is full of gratitude for everything God has given you ... even the trials ... then the joy comes.

As I continued to practice gratitude, that goodness spilled over into other areas of my life as well. I had more empathy for others and was less quick to judge or assume. My prayer life definitely improved, and I tried to start most days with scripture and a devotional to get my mind ready for whatever the day would hold. Surrounding myself with positivity helped me keep my troubles in check. I realized that things can always be worse and to be thankful for the troubles that I have. I no longer felt sorry for myself; I realized that even with the devastation that our family was dealing with, we were still extremely blessed.

Have you ever been around someone that is so negative that they *literally* drain the life out of you? They have a chip on their shoulder and take on the role of victim.

They are so blinded by their own troubles and sorrow that they fail to see the good that *is* in their life. Don't get me wrong, there are some folks that have suffered so much devastation in their life that you almost feel like they have *earned* a free pass to be hardened. Sometimes I look at my husband and all that he has lost in his life and I think that if he decided to be bitter I wouldn't blame him a bit. Thankfully my husband has worked through the loss and pain and will tell you real quick that he is blessed.

My mom has been a great example and role model for me as I have watched her over the years face so much adversity with strength and resilience. She has buried two husbands, was a single mom raising three kids for years, has lost a child, and watched both parents struggle and pass away after developing Alzheimer's. She has always picked herself back up and kept moving forward. She certainly could have developed a negative attitude over all that she has lost, but instead she made the decision to focus on the blessings and not on the loss. That is gratitude my friends.

Trust me when I say that I have tried it both ways. I have been so distraught over the years, and many times I wallowed in my heartache and pain. I wanted to blame God for allowing terrible things to happen to my family. I gave in to the victim mentality and let anger swallow me up. I could never find any peace in that frame of mind. When I finally surrendered all the brokenness and heartbreak to God admitting that I was angry but determined to find the silver lining in my situation, my mindset began to shift. Was it easy? No. It was quite difficult to let go of the despair and the need to blame someone, anyone, for the pain. But letting go was so freeing, and I felt the weight of it all literally fall off of me.

Start small if you have to, but the main thing is to start somewhere. Begin making a list today of everything that you are thankful for even if it seems small and silly. The idea is to get your mind in the habit of looking for the good in your life. Before you know it, it becomes second nature, and your entire perspective begins to change. You are able to let go of the need to blame others for the troubles in your life as you can see that the trials you're facing have not come to destroy you but instead to strengthen you and grow you spiritually.

Another wonderful way to practice gratitude is to take your mind off your own problems and reach out and help others. When you stop focusing on your own problems and help others in their time of need, it can also cause a shift in your mindset. Even doing something unexpected and nice for someone else can change their day and yours too. You realize how blessed you truly are. It can also help you see how far you have come! The act of putting others before yourself will shift your attitude to see that the grass on your side of the fence is green after all. It just needed to be watered.

I don't pretend to understand why things happen the way that they do. We live in a world that is full of good people with great intentions, but we also live in a fallen world that is full of sin. We can do everything "right" and still fall flat on our faces. Having gratitude even when it doesn't seem like there is much to celebrate in your life is the best attitude adjustment there is. It is hard to be bitter when you are full of gratitude.

We may not experience a problem-free existence, but let's face it, we *all* have troubles in life. Not one of us is going to get through life without having to face heartache and suffering at some point. We can open up our Bibles and read story after story of every day folks just like you and I that were faced with unthinkable adversity. They didn't always get it right either, but scripture shows us time and time again that a humble attitude full of praise and thanksgiving will take you far.

I believe without a doubt that gratitude is how and why I climbed out of the slimy pit of despair even though my circumstances did not change. If my happiness was dependent upon everything being perfect in my life, I might as well have given up a long time ago. There is no such thing as a perfect life, but practicing gratitude can definitely make what you already have be enough. I had to stop putting my happiness on hold as I waited for God to restore and replenish everything that enemy stole from my family. I decided to be happy anyway. Take that devil!

I am thankful that I had good role models and examples in my life. My mom, dad, and stepmom have always taught me to not let anything knock me down and keep me down. We have to fight through the heartbreak and pain no matter what. My sister-in-law told me one day that I could give myself a minute to wallow in my pain but I couldn't stay there. We have to pick ourselves up and brush ourselves off and keep moving forward. Remember, Earth is not our heaven. Our trouble-free life awaits us when God calls us home. So for now, we have to lean into God and let Him be our strength.

Find something to be grateful for today; don't wait for everything to be perfect in your life. If you do, you will be waiting a very long time. Be happy right in the middle of your mess, find joy in the simple things in life, and thank God for everything including the troubles. What if we were only given today what we were thankful for yesterday? That is a scary thought! Let's make sure we thank God for all His blessings but also for the lessons in life that have taught us how to be resilient when times are hard. I always say, God is good and life is hard, but when you have God, it is ALL good!

Colossians 3:16

"Let the word of Christ dwell in you richly in all wisdom: teaching and admonishing one another in psalms and hymns and spiritual songs, singing with grace in your hearts to the Lord."

Chapter 12

AMAZING GRACE

I think back on my life and I don't know how I would have made it this far if I had not had a relationship with Jesus. Life is *better* with Jesus, and I am not sure how folks survive it without Him. Parts of my testimony are sprinkled throughout this book, but I wanted to share more details in this chapter and also share a few other testimonies that are dear to my heart. We can go to church every Sunday, read our Bible from cover to cover, and quote scripture from memory, but I believe with all my heart that there is something so powerful in hearing another person's testimony about how they found Jesus.

I didn't grow up attending church every Sunday, so I am not really sure who introduced me to the big man upstairs. However, even as a small child, I talked to God on a regular basis. I never questioned His existence though I didn't know much about Him and knew nothing about the plan of salvation. All of that changed one day during my junior year in high school when my best friend shared her testimony with me. Hearing her tell about the Lord saving her soul made me realize that

I didn't have what she had and I *desperately* needed to find it.

I went a few weeks in that miserable condition of feeling lost. Finally at the end of my rope one night, I got down on my knees and prayed for God to help me. I begged Him to take away the heavy burden that weighed on my heart and save my soul. I surrendered everything to God in that very moment; I had reached the point of desperation and needed relief as I knew I was lost and separated from God.

The *moment* that God saved me I felt an *overwhelming* rush of peace and a tingling sensation that went from the top of my head to the bottom of my feet. I felt as light as air. The heavy burden was gone, and I had no doubt that I had just met Jesus. I felt the sweetest peace in my heart, and I slept better that night than I had in weeks. Salvation makes one fine pillow.

A few months after we got married, my husband got saved. Although my husband was raised in a Christian home and grew up going to church every Sunday, he did not find the Lord until he was twenty-five years old. He went to church every Sunday and was very knowledgeable about the Bible, but the knowledge was all in his head and not in his heart. He was a police officer working third shift, and I truly believe God worked on him during those long night shifts. My husband finally surrendered it all to God one evening in the little hallway of our rental house and was saved. God can save you anywhere you completely surrender your heart to Him.

I love to hear my husband share his testimony; it always brings me to tears. He went a very long time with only head knowledge of God. When he finally surrendered in that hallway calling on God, it became a heart matter. His salvation also changed the dynamic of our marriage significantly. Our marriage got better and grew stronger. God became the *glue* in our marriage. When things were hard, Jesus was what we had in common and always brought out the best in us. We both joined the church on the same day, we were baptized together in the creek, and that was when life truly began for both of us. It was the best thing that could have ever happened to us individually and for our marriage.

Fast forward several years to becoming a mom. I don't think you can start praying too soon for your children. During my pregnancies and throughout both of my children's lives, I have kept a daily prayer on my heart for their health, safety, future, and their spiritual walk. Even before they were born, I prayed that God would save their souls while they were young and tenderhearted and before the world could get a hold of them.

The Lord heard those prayers and so graciously answered them. On a hot and humid July morning in 2004, our family headed to church to attend revival. We were running late as usual, and I was rushing to get my youngest out of his car seat. My oldest son tugged on my skirt to get my attention, and what he said next stopped me in my tracks. He blurted out, "Mama! Jesus has just let go of me!" I turned to look at him, and for the first time in his seven and half years, I saw fear in his eyes. While the weight of his words was still sinking in, I grabbed the diaper bag and both kids, and we rushed into the church house.

I handed off my youngest to my mother-in-law and turned my attention to my oldest. He sat in the church pew with a hand motion like he was pushing something away and told me again, "Jesus is gone." My husband and I taught our children from a very young age that Jesus holds on to you when you are born, but we will all reach a point in our lives that He will let go of us and it's then our job to find our way back to Him through prayer. My son insisted that Jesus had left him on the car ride to church. Jesus was gone, our little boy was lost, and my heart was broken.

My husband came over to where we were sitting when he saw all the commotion going on. Our oldest told his dad about Jesus leaving him and that he knew he was lost. Soon our oldest son made his way up to the front of the church and kneeled down on the end of the altar. He bowed his head and began to pour out his little heart to the only one that could help him.

I felt the lowest I had ever felt in my life. As a parent, I was helpless because I knew that my little boy had to work out his own salvation. My husband and I had to step back, let go, and wait on the Lord. We both found a spot on the floor near the altar and knelt down to pour our hearts out to God. The whole church also went down in prayer. It wasn't long before our sweet boy poked his head up off the altar, and with the most precious smile on his face, told my husband, "Daddy I don't have to pray anymore, Jesus just saved me."

My husband and I jumped to our feet and almost tackled each other! We hugged, we cried, and we *shouted* the praises of God. My broken and heavy heart instantly filled with joy. A joy that is hard to describe. There is *nothing*, and I mean *nothing*, like hearing your child tell you that they have been saved. I feasted on those words for weeks and weeks. I told anyone who would listen how the Lord had graciously saved our son's soul. Our oldest joined the church that same day and was baptized a few days later in the creek with eight other beautiful souls.

Though relieved, I knew I had one child down but still had one to go. Let's just say that our youngest son is our strong willed and spirited child. As a toddler and young kid, he definitely kept us on our toes and quite possibly added a few gray hairs to our heads. He was incredibly funny, sweet, and cute as a button. He was also our little handful, and we quickly learned that he was a lot like the ocean; never turn your back on him.

Our youngest kept life interesting to say the least. During his first grade parent teacher conference, the teacher commented that our youngest definitely kept her entertained. In my mind I was thinking, "Oh dear, what has he said or done?" She then added, "He really loves the Lord and likes to pretend he is preaching on the playground." I let out a deep sigh of relief.

When our youngest was nine years old, I felt that he was getting close to the age of accountability by things he would say or ask us. I knew his salvation was between him and God, but I thought I might help him along. God would teach me a valuable lesson. It was my job to do the teaching and it was God's job to determine when and how to do the saving. God didn't need my help.

One day driving home from work, I had a very strong impression come over me that we "had run by" our youngest son's salvation. I laughed out loud a little because that didn't seem like a remote possibility. Our son was very vocal and could be a bit dramatic. I mean that in the best way possible. I didn't think there was *any* way that our youngest could have gotten saved and we *not* know about it.

A few days later, our family went Christmas shopping. As we were driving down the road, I began telling my husband about the strong feeling I had a few days prior in the car. My husband was driving, so he pulled down the rear-view mirror and asked our youngest, who was sitting right behind him, "Has the Lord ever saved your soul?" Our son's answer floored us both! Our youngest quickly replied, "Yes sir. He did, a month and a half ago, in my bed." My husband quickly pulled the vehicle over in an empty parking lot, and we both jumped out and ran to our son. Our youngest cried as he told us how the Lord had saved him all alone in his bed one night. I told you God didn't need my help.

Our youngest son told us that he had gone to bed that evening and a terrible feeling came over him. He said he knew immediately that he was lost. He told us that he started praying and asking God to save him. He didn't remember how much time went by, but after praying for a while, the trouble left and an unmistakable peace came into his heart. He told us he jumped up to come tell us the news but we were already asleep. Oh goodness, the one night that I wished he would have woken us up!

We rejoiced in the empty parking lot at the wonderful news. I felt a huge relief come over me. Both of my babies were saved and heaven bound! My circle was complete. I once again felt a feeling of joy that is hard to describe. Our youngest woke up the following Sunday morning, put on his little suit and clip-on tie, and joined the church during the service that day. He was baptized in the creek a short time later. There is *nothing* like hearing your child tell his testimony of being saved!

God answered two huge prayers that I had prayed while my babies were still in my belly. It was one of the prayers that I had persistently prayed their whole lives. Watching my boys go through all the motions of being lost, praying for God to save them, telling their experience of salvation, and then both joining the church and getting baptized increased my faith *tenfold*. I will *never* be able to adequately thank God for saving their souls while they were young boys.

After my kids got saved, it seemed like the Lord brought many opportunities for me and my husband to share our faith and take others to church with us to hear the gospel. My niece was one of those sweet experiences, and her testimony reminds me that God works everything out in His perfect timing.

After my oldest got saved, my niece, who is a few years older than him, really started asking my husband and me a lot of questions about God. She had heard all about our oldest getting saved and wanted to know what *she* needed to do to be saved.

A year after our oldest was saved on the altar at church, revival rolled back around. I decided to ask my oldest brother if we could take our niece to church with us. My brother and his family were going to the lake that day, but he agreed to meet us at a gas station close to church that evening so that we could take her with us. A few hours before church, I got a *very* strong impression to go buy my niece a dress and shoes for church. God was already at work!

Sure enough, my brother met us at the gas station to drop off my niece, and she climbed out of the car in her lake clothes, not exactly dressed for a church service. My brother apologized, but I told him not to worry, we had it covered. We made a makeshift dressing room in the back of our SUV while she changed into her "new" clothes. I brushed her hair, washed the lake off her with a wash cloth, and we headed to church a few miles down the road.

I had the strongest feeling in my heart that night that if I could just get her there, God was going to take care of everything. She sat next to me during the service, and soon the music started playing and the church began to sing. I glanced over at my niece only to see big tears falling down her cheeks. She looked up at me and asked if she could go to the altar to pray.

My niece got down on her knees at the altar and began to pour her heart out to God. She stayed on the altar for quite some time. The church went through many songs and several rounds of prayer as my husband and I sat in a pew close to the altar. All of a sudden, my niece lifted her head up off the altar with a huge smile on her face. She scanned the crowd of people before she spotted us and then jumped up and skipped over to tell us her wonderful news. The *whole* church rejoiced with her that night as we thanked God for saving another soul.

It was pretty late by this point, but my niece was bursting at the seams to tell her daddy the news. We drove her home, and when my brother answered the door, she jumped up in his arms and told him every detail of the night and how God had saved her soul. She had a smile on her face from ear to ear. My brother wiped the tears from his eyes as he gave her a big hug. Joy unspeakable once again!

Lying in bed later that night, I thanked God again for everything. I was so grateful that the Lord had watched over my niece, for saving her soul, and for putting all the moving parts together to be able to get her to church with us that night. I still get chills when I think about the strong impression God gave me that day to go buy her clothes for church. God knew how it would all come together, and I still get emotional thinking about it.

God has saved so many of my friends and family members over the years. As someone growing up outside of church, it became so important for me to share my own testimony with others. I have seen firsthand how God can take just a few words, plant the seed, and make a way for someone to be saved. I will never be able to thank Him enough for saving my boys, my niece, and so many others that I have had the honor and privilege to witness or even just hear their testimonies.

Salvation is our ticket to heaven. The plan of salvation is so simple that even a child can understand it. I think we sometimes make it too hard. Salvation is *peace* with God that comes at the end of a sincere and heartfelt prayer of complete surrender and repentance. It is something that you must work out for yourself, just you and God. I am so thankful for that. I would have never found it if it hadn't been simple.

God can save you anywhere. Philippians 2:12 says to *"work out your own salvation with fear and trembling."* My youngest brother got saved on the side of the road, my father-in-law was saved in an old pickup truck, my youngest was saved in his bed, one of my nephews was saved in our spare bedroom, and my dad got saved at fifty-six years old on an altar at church. My dad's testimony reminds me that it is never too late to find Jesus. I could go on and on listing all the places that I have heard people tell that the Lord saved them. Make an altar *somewhere* and pour your heart out to God. As long as you have breath in your body, it is never too late. Just ask!

I am so thankful that Jesus bore the cross and that anyone that calls upon His name, trusting and believing with all their heart, can be saved. I have heard some people say that they have done too much bad in their life for God to save their souls. Not possible! Jesus can save anyone that surrenders their heart to Him, even the rankest of sinners. He hung on that cruel cross for *all* of mankind. You just need childlike faith.

After I got saved, I didn't instantly pick up my Bible and run out to find a church to attend. That came years later. I was saved, but I definitely did not cultivate my relationship with God, and I missed out on blessings. When I met my husband and started attending church with him, I finally began to build my relationship with God, and not only that, but I began to grow in my faith. I loved going to church each Sunday to hear the beautiful hymns, listen to the preaching, and soak in all the beautiful testimonies of God's people.

I hope that anyone that hasn't been saved will consider Jesus. Ask yourself this important question, "Where am I going when I die?" If you have never been saved, make an altar somewhere and call out to Him from your heart to save your soul. There is no "canned" prayer or magical words; it is a humble prayer from your heart to God's ears. God *knows* the condition of our hearts, so we must come to Him humble and sincere. I believe He hears and answers when we fully repent and surrender. Peace comes in and the trouble is gone. You won't have to be told, you will know for yourself!

There is not a single person on this earth that can look into the heart of a lost sinner and tell them when they have repented enough. That is God's job. We can tell others how we got saved, we can encourage and pray for them, but we have to leave the saving to Him. As a mom, that was hard for me. I had to let go of my children and trust that they would find their own way. Let me add, you *can* trust your children with God. As much as I love my kids, God loves them even more.

When the Lord saves you, be *sure* to share your testimony with others. I am so thankful that our

youngest finally told us about being saved. Worrying about him was hard, and without him sharing his testimony with us, we would have never known.
Your salvation is your ticket to heaven, and when you leave this world, your testimony is the peace of mind that you offer to your family and friends that it is not "goodbye" but "see you later." Psalm 107:2 says, *"Let the redeemed of the Lord say so."* Don't hide it; share it with everyone you can!

I hope this chapter of testimonies warms your heart and helps someone that is searching or even confused. Keep seeking Him friend; James 4:8 says, *"Draw nigh to God, and he will draw nigh to you."* Salvation is the greatest gift you will ever receive on this side of eternity, and like I said before, it is your ticket to your "heavenly home." Most importantly, don't ever give up until you know He saved you. Some people get saved the first time they pray, others may spend years seeking the Lord. We can't figure it out in our minds; we have to take a leap of faith into the arms of our savior and trust Him with our whole heart.

I will never be able to thank Him enough for making a way for me. I knew nothing about God when I heard my friend give her testimony at school that day. I had limited head knowledge of Him, but when I felt the conviction hit me that day at school, it became a matter of the heart. I spent a few weeks searching for Him, and then one night, down on my knees, I let go of this world. I couldn't carry the burden any longer, and I surrendered every thought, every worry, and basically everything I had. That is when the work was done for me. That is when God replaced trouble in my heart with sweet salvation.

We can help others by sharing our testimony with them. Be willing to share your story and believe that God will use it to help others make their way to Him. Never be afraid or ashamed to share what God has done in your life. For those that doubt our testimonies, leave that in God's hands too. God doesn't need us to try and convince anyone, He simply needs our willingness to share our own experience. Leave the convicting and convincing to Him.

I often hear that folks don't want to surrender their life to God because they can't have fun anymore or won't be able to live good enough. Scripture reminds us that none of us are good enough. In Romans 3:10, *"There is none righteous, no, not one."* Christian and non-Christians alike make mistakes and will continue to make mistakes. The good news is that Jesus has already paid the penalty for all of our sins. Salvation doesn't make you *perfect*, it makes you *forgiven*.

Don't put it off; seek Him while He can be found. When He saves you, make sure you tell someone the wonderful news!

John 3:16–17

"For God so loved the world, that he gave his only begotten Son, that whosoever believeth in him should not perish, but have everlasting life. For God sent not his Son into the world to condemn the world; but that the world through him might be saved."

Ephesians 2:8–9

"For by grace are ye saved through faith; and that not of yourselves: it is the gift of God: Not of works, lest any man should boast."

Acknowledgements

This book was written to bring honor and glory to God. I would not have made it through this life without His mercy and grace. I am just a sinner saved by His marvelous grace.

My husband Chris, you are my hero and I love you more each day. Thank you for not telling me I was crazy when I said I was publishing a book. I want to thank you for always being my biggest cheerleader and encouraging me when I wanted to quit.

My boys, Caleb and Isaac, you two are my heart and soul. I am so proud of both of you. When life got hard for our family overnight, you both kept the faith and motivated Mama to not give up. I love you both more than you will ever know.

Alexis and Aubrey Lynn, I am so happy to finally have girls in the family! I love you both to the moon and back! You have both brought so much joy into my life.

To my parents, Sue Carr and Les and June Hinton, your unwavering support and love means more to me than you will ever know. I have the best parents in the world; your love saw me through the hardest season in my life. Thank you for the pep talks when I didn't think I could make it another day.

My in-laws, Dean and Joyce Cline. I could never have handpicked better in-laws. You two are godsent, and I love you both. Thank you for loving me like your own.

Cathy and Avoe (Sister and Little Sister), I love you both so much and appreciate your love and unwavering support.

To my siblings, Julie, Jeff, Don, Andy, and Scott, I love you all, and I am thankful to be your sister.

To my sisters-in-law, Cricket, Kim, and Theresa, I love each one of you, and I am beyond grateful that my brothers found God-fearing and loving women to spend their lives with. Brother Tim, I love you too and thank you for loving my sister as Christ loves the church.

Taylor and Sydney, your daddy would be so proud of you both, and I hope you know Aunt LaLa is always here to cheer you on.

My bestie, Kim Bowen, you are my ride or die, my free therapist, and my sister in Christ. I thank God for you every day! Thank you for sharing Jesus with me so many years ago, it changed my life forever.

Kathy Mackison (Coach Krazy Kat), you saw something in me that I could not see in myself. You are a huge reason I found the courage to put my story on paper and write this book. Thank you sweet friend for the support and encouragement you gave me along the way.

Acknowledgements

To our church families and praying friends, we appreciate you more than you will ever know. Your prayers and love sustained us during the hardest time in our lives. God bless each one of you!

To all those that helped me get this book to print, I am so grateful for each of you holding my hand and making this dream a reality.

About the Author

Laurie Cline is an author in the collaborative anthology book and #1 Best Seller, Fiercely Faithful. She is passionate about writing and sharing her story and hopes to encourage others to choose joy during difficult seasons in life. She has been married to Chris for twenty-six years; they have two children, Caleb and Isaac, a daughter-in-law, Alexis, and one granddaughter, Aubrey Lynn.

Can You Help?

THANK YOU FOR READING MY BOOK!

I really appreciate all of your feedback, and I love hearing what you have to say.

I need your input to make the next version of this book and my future books better.

Please leave me an honest review on Amazon letting me know what you thought of the book.

Much love and many blessings!

Laurie Cline

Made in the USA
Columbia, SC
30 May 2021